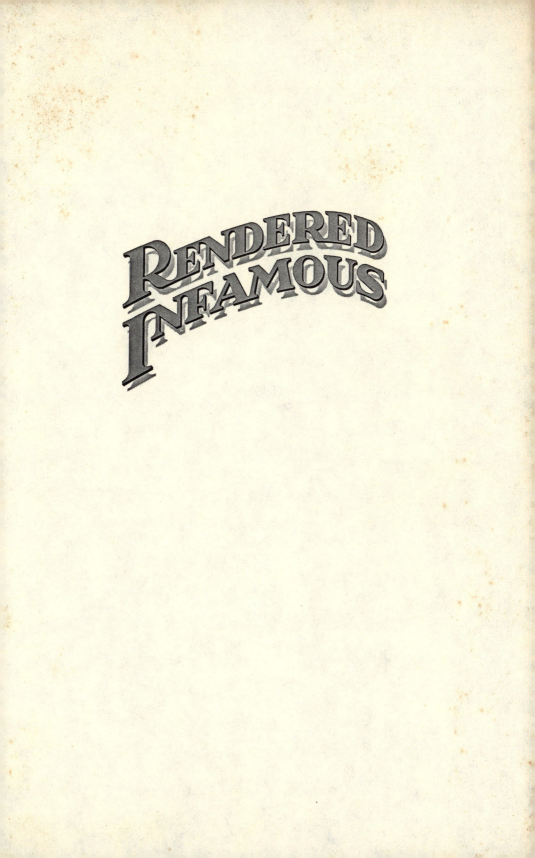

RENDERED INFAMOUS

A BOOK OF POLITICAL REALITY

RENDERED INFAMOUS

by

STEPHEN GASKIN

THE BOOK PUBLISHING COMPANY
Summertown, Tennessee

First printing.

Manufactured in the United States.

Library of Congress Catalog Card #81-70392
Gaskin, Stephen
Rendered Infamous

ISBN #0-913990-40-X

Contents

Dedication

I want to dedicate this book to Nashville, Tennessee. I mean, it's really to everybody, but it's especially dedicated to Nashville. It's a letter to my friends and neighbors, the Tennesseans, who took us in.

Some of this book is about Korea. Some of it is about politics. And some of it is about the Tennessee State Penitentiary.

The penitentiary is yours. You are the people who are the landlords. You are the public service department, you are the corrections department. And what is in this book about the Walls is for you.

First Political Memories

My first political memory is the fall of Czechoslovakia in 1939. I was four years old, sitting in the bathtub, tearing up a green sponge rubber monkey, when my Aunt Margie walked into the bathroom, saw me pulling the stuffing from the green rubber monkey, and said,

"Don't tear up that monkey. That monkey was made in Czechoslovakia, and Czechoslovakia fell today; there may not ever be anything again that comes out with the label, 'Made in Czechoslovakia'."

The beginning of World War II, the attack on Pearl Harbor, is very clear to me. My family was driving in the mountains above Denver, as we frequently did on weekends, with some soldiers from Lowry Field, of the Army Air Force, before the Air Force was separate, whom we had picked up hitchhiking. Drinking a few beers, beautiful Colorado Rockies. We pulled into Colorado Springs, and the extra editions of the newspapers were on the street. It said WAR in letters that went from the top of the page to the bottom of the page.

As the newsboy handed the paper through the window into the car, the ink was wet, and my mother's fingers smeared that word. December 7, 1941.

By 1943, my father was working at Camp Hale, Colorado, an Army ski-trooper training base in a 10,000 foot valley known only as the Pando Railroad Crossing. Camp Hale was the home of a German prisoner of war camp. When we first arrived, the prisoners had been captured from Rommel's Afrika Korps. Tall and sunburned, with sun-bleached eyebrows, strong and heavy looking. But later in the war, as the push through France and towards Germany carried through, the prisoners became old men and young boys—sixteen years, fourteen years old—as the Germans were taking the last available manpower to send out for their war.

In adjoining barbed wire enclosures identical to those of the German prisoners, they kept the conscientious objectors. They were called "620's." I never found out why; I think it was the number of the law that referred to them. Conscientious objectors were presumed to be disloyal because they wouldn't fight. They were locked in identical barbed wire enclosures with the same guards as the German soldiers. They were stranger to me than the German soldiers. I understood the German soldiers. I wondered if the conscientious objectors were spies.

I was well-equipped with hate, 1941-style. For Hitler, Tojo, Il Duce. The cartoons and posters—"Loose lips sink ships"; Hitler with his ever-present salute and his black bang hanging over one eye; Tojo drawn as racist as possible with round little eyeglasses and buck teeth; and Il Duce, large jaw and pointed head, comically puffed chest full of medals. The villains were plain, and the issues seemed simple, most of the time.

One of the German prisoners had the job of walking through the civilian housing for the secretaries and office staff for the camp, knocking the icicles off the edges of the roof before they got so big they dragged down the eaves. A ski trooper base in a valley at ten thousand feet.

Another prisoner seemed particularly kind and friendly, and was introduced to me by his guard. I was told, "This is Karl."

Later on, late at night, with my ear to the crack of my bedroom door, I listened to my parents talk about Karl with the stud card. He had been judged a perfect specimen of the Master Race. He had been given a card which instructed all sufficiently Aryan women to cooperate and bear children by this perfect Aryan specimen. The reason Karl was a trusty, and was allowed to work in the civilian housing area, was because he had surrendered on purpose. The lady he loved was short and dark, and didn't look Aryan at all; and he was forbidden to consider her as a mate. He turned against the Nazi philosophy, although he could have been one of the beneficiaries of that system. He talked freely with his guard about Germany, and what it was like under Hitler; and it wasn't as simple as the posters of Hitler and Tojo and Il Duce.

The German soldiers, like prisoners everywhere, pursued the path of something to ease the feelings of jail, and built themselves a still inside the wall, with no parts more than four inches wide. They carried home pockets of raisins and sugar from the mess hall, and made raisin jack, and occasionally had parties and got drunk and sang German songs.

While we were still at Camp Hale, my father was offered another government job at Tucson, Arizona. It was similar kind of work, as housing manager. We loaded up our old '39 Cadillac while they were tearing down Camp Hale, and took off for Tucson. When we arrived, we couldn't find a motel that was open for us to check into. My father, in one of those impulses which I have seen him do, which gave me hope and let me know there was free will, said,

"If Tucson doesn't want us, we don't want Tucson. Let's go to California."

We filled up in a filling station in Tucson and moved on out to California, where houses were cheap and boats were cheap. People were afraid of the Japanese invading the coast of California.

We lived in a fine old beach house where I could stand out on the beach sometimes and watch blimps and PBYs hunting submarines between Catalina and the coast. Oil would wash up on the beach from naval battles we never heard of. The soldiers would come down the beach walk, knocking on each door where a light was shown and telling them the blackout's on, close your shades, put out that light.

While I hunkered in the front yard out of sight, watching the soldiers go by without them suspecting I was there, I saw a soldier with a little red flower pot three inches high stuck in the netting in the top of his helmet, with a little paper flower sticking out the top. Fitting camouflage for a Southern California soldier.

My mother was out driving, and picked up a young flyboy on crutches, with casts on leg and arm. She asked him, "Where did you get your wounds, son? Were you hurt in Europe, or were you out in the Islands?"

He said, "No, ma'am. I wasn't in Europe or the Islands either. I just tore out three telephone poles and a hundred and fifty feet of wire with a P-38."

One time when I was a little boy, visiting with my grandparents back in Texas, I went to the oilfields with my Aunt Margie and her boyfriend, Alex, in Alex's fine yellow convertible. We parked beside an old oil derrick. Margie and Alex got out to look at it, and told me to stay in the car. In those days in Texas, much of the oil was close to the ground and under artesian pressure. While I sat in the car watching the crew working around the edge of the derrick, there was a sudden roar and the earth shook, and just like they say in the old cartoons, up come a gusher.

A six inch shaft of crude oil shot to the top of the derrick and shattered and splashed against the monkey board on the top and bent over at the top like the spout of a right whale, and rained down black crude oil all over and Aunt Margie and Alex threw their arms around one another and kicked and danced and jumped up and down.

I saw a piece of the American dream, watching a gusher come in.

My grandmother was running a boarding house for servicemen's wives in Newport Beach, California, and there were servicemen from all the nearby bases. That was okay. There was not much question of rank; it was mostly just the women. But on Christmas, their husbands all came, and they had a Christmas party there at the house. There was a major and a few lieutenants, and some high master sergeants and tech sergeants, and some lower ranks, some corporals and such, too. At some point in the evening, one of the officer's wives got a little hancty with one of the enlisted men's wives about being married to an officer and all. My grandmother, who had been preparing the holiday dinner, came out of the kitchen with her apron on and said,

"I want you to know that in this house there ain't but one rank, and that rank is *mine*. And that outranks all these other ranks in here. So I am going to take all these ranks off." She went around to all the officers and unpinned their insignia off their collars. She took their oak leaves and their railroad tracks and all that, and went over and piled them up in a little pile on the mantel and said,

"Now there is no rank in this house."

I've been exposed to that stuff since youth, and it may have made its mark on me. My grandmother was a suffragette, and was in the streets for the women's vote. I saw a picture of her in her suffragette suit, which was pretty severe. She always wore pants and slacks and stuff well after many of her daughters were pretty wealthy and moved in pretty high social class. She made her own pantsuits and said, "I wear pants."

My greatgrandfather was a socialist, and voted for Eugene V. Debs—Samuel Gompers wouldn't support him, because he was too leftwing and antiestablishment. The Pullman strike wound up with Debs versus J. P. Morgan himself in the Supreme Court of the United States; and the Supreme Court had to decide that Debs was right, because to side with Morgan would have established too strong a precedent for governmental protection of "free enterprise"—they couldn't exactly say that Morgan's interests, those of a private corporation, were identical with the country's. Later they put Debs in jail for opposing the war. He got over a million votes for President while he was still locked up. Debs said,

"You have power. They let you vote. Vote."

He also said, "As long as anyone is in jail, I am not free."

My uncle was a union organizer in San Francisco, and helped organize the waterfront in the days of Harry Bridges.

When we left California, we went back to New Mexico, to
Santa Fe, because there was said to be a big project there,
lots of work, plenty of stuff to do. We went to Santa Fe, and
my father helped build the Los Alamos atomic plant,
previous to Hiroshima.

My father and my aunt and uncle all worked in the plant.
My father came home and told us they were sure doing
something wild up there—they had huge earth dams in
between the buildings. Then one night, all the people of New
Mexico who were awake in the middle of the night thought
the sun was rising at an early hour as a bright glow came up
off the desert at Alamogordo, New Mexico, as the first bomb
off its tower fused the desert floor into glass. We didn't know
what it was, but we knew something had happened in New
Mexico. Then it happened in Hiroshima. Then it happened in
Nagasaki. Then we knew what it was.

I have another clear political memory, at ten years old,
riding around the plaza in Santa Fe, New Mexico, firing my
cap pistols out the window, in a long procession of cars with
horns honking, people dancing, singing in the streets: it was
the end of the war with Japan.

The closeness of the atomic plant remained part of my
consciousness for the rest of my life, as it does today. In
Santa Fe, you have to pass the high school to get from Los
Alamos out of state. We always heard the stories of the
traffic from Los Alamos. There was a long downgrade, and
the Santa Fe Federal Building was at the bottom of the
downgrade, at a T in the highway. Many cars coming down
that grade went through the fence onto the lawn of the
Federal Building. One day a truck from Los Alamos wrecked
at "Tombstone T"—the New Mexico equivalent of Dead
Man's Curve. The secret team from the plant came down the
twenty-four miles of mountain road from Los Alamos in
twenty-five minutes.

I remember standing in the playground of the high school,
watching a caravan of six black Buick sedans with three FBI
agents in the front seat and three FBI agents in the back
seat, and shotguns and submachine guns laid up on the

rear window ledge, and then one small government, olive-drab square truck that looked like a bread truck, and six more black Buick sedans with three FBI agents in front and three FBI agents in back, with submachine guns and shotguns. When we saw them go by, the high school kids in my school said,

"There goes an atomic bomb."

We knew what they were.

A good friend of mine, one of my high school friends, a young hunting friend—we used to stroll in the brush with our .22 rifles and plink—named Harold, had been out in the desert and had brought home a strange rock. At first we thought it was a rock, but then as we looked closer, we saw that not only did it have strange properties, but that it was obviously *made*, not natural rock. It looked as if it was the broken section of a large doughnut, fourteen or fifteen inches across, perhaps, with a hole in the middle, about four inches thick. It was a piece of a doughnut about the size of a football. Its mass was eighty-five pounds.

It was uncanny to see something so heavy for its size. If you tried to pick it up, it tended to roll off the side of your hand towards your little finger: it was so heavy it tended towards the place of least resistance. Strong men would pick it up and try to hold it over their head. It was dark, gunmetal grey, with many-sided crystals on the broken edges, and the marks of some kind of casting on the made edges. It had a slight crack, and we used a sledge hammer to knock off a small chip at the cracked place, about the size of a fifty cent piece. The chip was so hard that it cut glass as if it were a glass cutter. That was the only chip we were able to break loose from it. We beat it with a sledge hammer until the sledge hammer was beaten back into the shape of a mushroom. We tried to burn it. We propped up an oxyacetylene cutting torch on a couple of bricks with the blue tip of the cutting flame touching the surface, and went away and had lunch. We came back an hour later, and there was a small, cherry-red glow the size of a quarter. But we couldn't burn it.

People from the neighborhood would come to see it—

"Hey, let's see that funny rock you've got there, Harold!"

We showed it off, and showed them how sharp the chip was.

Then one day a black Buick with red, white and blue Federal government license plates and two men in conservative suits, one dark green, one dark brown, with snap brim hats, took our rock and placed it in a lead box in the trunk of the Buick, giving us no receipt, no sayso, and drove away with it.

Here ends the first person section of this encounter. The remaining portions are hearsay and circumstantial. You can judge for yourself.

Later on, an aunt of mine had an executive secretarial position at Los Alamos, in the office of medical research. She said she found among the records in her workload a file about Harold's funny rock, which said it was eighty-five pounds of uranium oxide, and that it was missing from Los Alamos, and that at some level those people who had come in contact with it had been monitored to see if they had any ill effects from it.

This part of the story becomes more convoluted. Many years later, as the atomic weapons and power industry continued to flower, I began to realize the import of these encounters. I began correspondence with the federal government under the Freedom of Information Act. I wrote to various government agencies on various letterheads, as I was instructed to do by return mail. Finally, at the end of a long and fruitless search, I was told that none of those records were available. I gave them the name of the doctor who had compiled the files, the name of the secretary who had filed them, the name of the people who had found the rock, a sufficiency of information for a file known to be in existence. I was unable, through the Freedom of Information Act, to obtain any information from the government on this question.

Due to family pressures, I am forbidden to hassle my aunt, who is old and whose pension derives from her work at Los

Alamos.

I thought I had to leave it there, so I wrote a sort of cute sarcastic letter to the people at the Freedom of Information Bureau that said I would be willing to forget the whole thing if it weren't for the black Buick with the red white and blue license plates and the lead box in the trunk, for which I received no answer.

Still later, I met Michio Kaku, a young atomic physicist who had been a student radical at Berkeley. He said he would never use his knowledge of physics to build weapons, but he would try to bring knowledge of physics to the people. He was one of the first non-industry physicists allowed inside Three Mile Island to assess the true damage.

I told him my story and he said,

"My, that sounds like a part being assembled for a bomb."

He said the description of the substance and its properties were accurate, and once again I had to think.

Later still, I met Ted Lombard, one of the men who assembled the bombs used in World War II. I told him my story, and he told me,

"That was part of a bomb. I used to make bombs out of pieces like that. They told me it was okay to handle it with your bare hands," and he held his hands out for me to see. His fingers were swollen and split in places, and oozing and crusting. He looked into my eyes and said,

"They haven't healed since 1945."

He told me of the birth defects of his children and his grandchildren.

So even if they won't tell me, I know what I had. And I know something else that most people in this country don't get to know for sure, and I will tell you this:

The government lies.

Boot Camp

The recruiting posters advertise that the Marine Corps is full of great physical specimens. The way I got into the Marine Corps was that I went to the Air Force first and said I wanted to join the Air Force, and was just flat told by the Air Force recruiting officer that nobody with 20/400 vision in one eye and 20/200 vision in the other eye is going to become a pilot or is very likely to ever set foot in an airplane.

So I thought perhaps I would join the Marine Corps, because I didn't think vision would be such a factor. The minimum weight in the Marine Corps at the time was 115 pounds. When I joined, I was six feet even and weighed 116 pounds. So they weren't real particular.

They were less particular than that. They were drafting people. A lot of the guys I went in with were draftees.

Going in and signing up with the oath and all that was actually pretty good, but the thing that first made me know that I might possibly have made a mistake was when we all went down and got on the train to boot camp in San Diego. After we were all seated, the door at each end of the car was locked, and an armed guard, holding his rifle in front of him in his hands, was stationed at the door at each end of the train car. We were put under guard as much as if we were criminals.

I had thought that the military was like the movies or the books; I had brought a deck of cards and some dice and a couple of games to play, because I figured there would be hours of time to while away and wanted to have some cards to play or something. On having my shaving kit searched by the drill sergeant, I was immediately assumed to be a card shark and a hustler, and I was treated as if I had been some kind of sharpie who was going to come in and run some heavy games and make a lot of money somehow. They took my stuff away.

It was four-thirty in the morning, and we were told to make our beds. We made regulation military beds which took up half the remaining time we had to sleep, getting up for the first time to hear Sergeant Padilla, who called himself Padilla without the Spanish pronunciation of the double-l, because that's the way the Marine Corps is. He told us we were lower than whale shit, and whale shit is at the bottom of the ocean; that there was nothing lower than whale shit, except us. We were not civilians any more, and we did not have the freedoms or rights of a civilian, so we could kiss that goodbye, and we were *certainly* not Marines, and that many of us couldn't even *be* Marines, wouldn't be able to make it. Many of us would fail, and the remainder of us could possibly be whipped into shape, but he doubted it seriously.

The clothes we were issued were too large to fit. At the time, I just thought they issued us clothes that were too large to be mean to us and make us look funny. But then I realized that they expected us to gain weight, and they were trying to fit us for the size we were going to be at the end of boot camp. I did gain nineteen pounds in boot camp, for sheer survival. I ate everything I could get my hands on, washing it down with a large pint-and-a-half bowl of cream of wheat after a breakfast of bacon and eggs and sausage and toast. Anything to try to get myself strong enough to not just be wasted by the life we lived.

With our hair cut off, the tops of our ears sunburned until they bled. We thought it was a disease.

The first night in our barracks, Quonset huts in San Diego, next door to the airfield where B-36's were built and tuned, I was given a flashlight and told I was firewatch, and told to watch our company's street. It was almost the first time I had had to be peaceful and alone, in the middle of the night.

As I walked down the street, I came past the end door of the Quonset hut where the drill instructors lived. I heard a sudden burst of shouting and scratching inside the door, and suddenly the door opened in front of me endways from the top down, and fell, torn off equally from lock and hinges, and lay in the company street with a bright shaft of yellow light across it and a young marine about my age lying on the door, who had just been thrown through a closed door.

I stopped in shock, until the drill instructor said,

"What are you looking at, clown? You'd better get out of here, shithead."

That's what drill instructors call you instead of Grasshopper.

I turned and resumed my walk, understanding that, although I was the watchman, that was not the sort of thing I was supposed to watch for.

One of the other boots was an efficient and together sort of fellow, and I tried to befriend him. He turned from where he sat cleaning his rifle, which always gleamed, in his boot uniform which already looked comfortable on him while the rest of us still looked like sacks, and said,

"I intend to be honor man in this platoon, and I don't want anything to be around me that will keep me from being honor man. I don't like you, and I want you to stay away from me."

I understood that some people took this Marine business very seriously. Much more seriously than I did, I could tell right away.

All the physical training, all the bayonet training, all the judo training, all the obstacle courses, did me no good whatsoever. I went back to Santa Fe on my boot leave and ran into the same bully who had beaten me up five times all the way through high school. He took one look at my Marine Corps uniform, and proceeded to beat me up again, just to show me where it was really at.

Most of the stuff that went on in boot camp I could consider something like college hazing, and although it was tiring and obscene and profane, it didn't usually seem cruel to me, except in the case of Sanchez, a married man with a couple of children. I have no idea why they took him in the Marine Corps.

He was short, strong and well-built, and he had obviously worked hard all his life, but he wasn't very tall, and his uniform hung on him, and they called him Satchel Ass. They loaded all the pockets of his uniform and his field transport pack with rocks, maybe a hundred pounds, maybe more. They made him walk at the end of the platoon and derided him, jeered at him, called him Satchel Ass, and put him to shame for not keeping up, because he was short, and Mexican.

Some of us were punk kids who needed shaped up, I suppose. But the Marine Corps couldn't tell the difference, and serious, heavy family people were treated lightly.

It's like a friend of mine once said in the penitentiary,

"Stone walls and steel bars do not a prison make. But you throw in some bad food and bad mattresses, obnoxious guards and a general lack of amenities, and you've got something."

Several times during the course of our boot training, we were asked to collect money to buy expensive presents for the drill instructors. Hundreds of dollars were collected from us during the time we were in boot camp, and given to drill instructors, either as cash or in the form of expensive radios—in those days, a Zenith Transoceanic was the standard—but I never understood where our drill instructor was really at until I ran into him on the deck of the *General W. H. Gordon* headed for Korea, and looked at the ribbons on his chest, and saw that, like me, he hadn't been out of the United States either, that this was his first trip to combat, same as mine. We looked in each other's eyes, and the difference between drill instructor and boot melted completely away, because I knew he didn't really know anything more than I did; we were both going into combat for the first time.

13-B-6

When I left boot camp, before going to Korea, my first duty station was fourteen months as a Marine prison guard at 13-B-6, the Camp Pendleton stockade, rumored to be one of the Marine Corps' most intense prison facilities. On my first day in, walking among the army tents surrounded with barbed wire, I saw one of the prisoners with a several-days' growth of beard. I was curious as to why he had the beard—at no time did I think he was trying to sneak in having a beard; I understood that the Marine Corps was tight enough that no one was going to get by without shaving for more than a day. I said,

"Hey, whatcha doing? Growing a beard?"

He turned to me with real fear in his eyes. I was six feet tall and weighed a hundred thirty-five pounds. No one had *ever* been afraid of me. But this grown-up looking man turned to me with real fear in his eyes and began to stutter, and tried to explain that he had a note from the doctor, to forestall any cruel thing I might do to him. I realized that this was a place where people did things to people, and I was on the side of the people who did things.

I never hit anyone, but I did things that, when I look back on them now, seem so childishly and pompously cruel as to make me ashamed. I had the men in one tent arrange their beds in such a fashion that when I came through their tent in the morning, banging on the ends of their iron bed frames with my twenty-four inch billy club, that the bed frames played "Mary Had a Little Lamb."

Things in the stockade went two ways. I probably was only getting my just deserts when I was letting myself out of one of the smaller cages by reaching through the bars with my keys and unlocking the gate from the outside, when one of the trusties walked up and said,

"Here, let me unlock that for you."

He took the keys out of my hand and walked away with them, and left me locked up inside, about ten-thirty at night.

"Come back here with those keys!"

"Hee-hee-hee, come get me!"

"You come back here with those keys, right this minute!"

"You just come and get 'em if you want 'em."

I went for the barbed wire fence, and began scaling up over the fence. I was about three feet off the ground when I heard the sound of a rifle bolt clack above my head from the guard tower behind my back. I heard the guard in the tower say,

"Get down off that fence."

"Hey, man, I'm a guard! Let me out of here! That sucker's got my keys!"

"*Get...down...off...that...fence!*"

"Hey, man, come on..."

"*Shut up, and get down off that fence!*"

I climbed back down the fence and looked at the trusty, who held the keys out to me tantalizingly for a few more moments and then, before another guard was dispatched to sort out our situation, unlocked the gate and gave me back my keys.

I always wondered if the guy in the tower would have shot, if I had kept climbing the fence. There was no way to tell from how he sounded. Sometimes the guards said they wanted a chance to shoot a prisoner, because you got a transfer if you did.

I remember taking a prisoner from the military brig to a hearing that happened to be on a Sunday. We took a shortcut through the warehouses, and I found myself alone with a prisoner some years older than I, walking in front of my shotgun on a long, empty company street with all the warehouse doors closed, a block-long tunnel with nobody but him and me. Right in the middle, he stopped and turned around and said,

"What would you do if I ran?"

I looked at him with true fear in my heart. I pointed the shotgun skyward and moved the pump to jack the shell into the chamber; but I stayed with the gun pointing toward the sky. The prisoner walked up close to me and looked deep into my eyes and studied my face.

"Naw, you're too young and skittish. You might even do it. Okay, never mind. Let's go."

And he turned around and walked in front of me to his appointment.

I didn't think I was a bad guard at the time; I honestly thought I was a pretty good guard at the time. But that was only in comparison to a lieutenant who took over command of our company for a short time. He was a big, handsome man with iron grey temples. He had been division boxing champ, judo champ, wrestling champ at one time or another. He had one of the highest intelligence scores recorded in the Marine Corps, and would have been something magnificent if it weren't for a twisted and cruel streak that went through his makeup.

We had all heard the rumors of the MP's hauling him back from Oceanside, tearing up bars, sliding by punishment again and again in recognition of his war record. But I discovered what he could be like one night when I was the guard in solitary.

Most of the prison section was made out of army tents with barbed wire twelve feet high around them; but solitary was made of two-by-fours laid flat, so the walls were four inches thick, solid two-by-fours, with screens across the top and a catwalk above for a guard to walk on, about eight cells on each side of the aisleway. I was standing duty late at night when the lieutenant let himself in the door. He walked to me and stopped in front of me. I stood at attention, looking straight ahead as a junior enlisted man is expected to in the presence of an officer. The lieutenant said,

"About face."

I tapped one toe behind the other heel and spun smartly in a crisp, military about-face.

"Forward, march!" the lieutenant ordered.

I marched forward until it looked as if I was going to run into the wall at the end of the building, at which time the lieutenant called me to a "Halt! One-two!" which left me standing with my nose a bare three inches from the wall at the end of the room.

The lieutenant followed me to the end of the room, and lifted the keys to the solitary confinement cells. I could smell the whiskey on his breath as he took the keys from my belt. He walked back to the front, to the first cell, and opened the door.

The prisoner stood at attention inside the door of the cell, as were the orders for solitary confinement, and the lieutenant said,

"You think you're pretty tough, don't you?"

"No, sir," said the prisoner.

The lieutenant's fist shot out, striking him in the stomach, knocking him against the back wall of the cell. The lieutenant slammed the door and locked it, and continued to the second cell.

The prisoner stood at attention in the doorway of the cell while the lieutenant taunted him a few taunts, and then knocked him back into the cell.

The lieutenant went along through all the cells, striking each man. No answer was acceptable. "No sir," "Yes sir," both received a blow.

After the last cell was closed, the lieutenant said,

"About *face*."

I faced about.

"Did you see anything, boy?" the lieutenant asked.

I was seventeen years old, and I weighed a hundred thirty-five pounds; and he was the division boxing and wrestling champion.

"No sir," I said.

I later told my story, and several other guys told theirs,

and the lieutenant was transferred to another outfit; but nothing serious ever happened to him. The Marine Corps, like the doctors, protect their own.

Korea

When I arrived in Able Company, First Battallion, Fifth
Marine Regiment, Second Platoon, and came into our
thirteen-man olive-drab squad tent, they pointed out an
empty cot as my bunk. While I started unpacking my gear,
unrolling my sleeping bag, and making up my bed to lay
down to sleep—it was already nighttime—there was some
jive and argument going on among the men in the tent. My
bunk was next to the end of the line. The guy in the bunk at
the end of the line said to someone across the tent,

"I already shot somebody today; maybe I'll just shoot you
if you don't watch it."

The tent froze. The vibes turned ugly—angry, and mean.
One of the guys got up off his bunk and walked over,
shouting past me at that dude like I wasn't even there, like I
was a piece of furniture or a tree, that he'd better shut up and
mind his business, and he'd better stay over in his corner by
himself and not talk to any other people in the tent, and if he
said another word to anybody, the guy might kill him. The
vibes were so bad that it sounded feasible; he might.

I just shrank back on my bed and kept my mouth *shut*.

In the course of the conversation that went on among the
other guys in the tent, it seemed that the fellow at the end
had had an incident happen. He said he had dropped his
Browning Automatic Rifle, and it jammed and fired its entire
magazine through this other guy's body, twenty shots of
heavy rifle fire. All the other guys swore that you couldn't

jam a BAR that way, and that he must have held the trigger down himself. Nobody of the troops believed the guy's story that the BAR jammed. The authorities were in a position of being unable to prove anything.

The guy was transferred out that night. I don't know where he was sent or whether he stood trial, or what. He was just transferred out of where we were.

That was my first vibrational acquaintance with death and I could tell the flavor of real death.

I was transferred into a different platoon for some reason several days later; and the first night I was in that platoon, they came back from somewhere and I was understandably a little shy and afraid to hit on them too much from what my other platoon had been like. I asked them where they had been, and they said, "On patrol."

I asked if they had seen any combat, and Munoz, a funny, intelligent cat from Colorado who the other guys called sheepherder, started this long funny monologue about how "I slew thousands with my rifle, and when my rifle failed to function freely, I took my entrenching tool and held off the charge; and when my entrenching tool failed to function freely, I took my rifle cleaning tool and yet fought the fight." It was pretty funny, pretty good vibes, and a relief from what it had been like to be around a platoon where most of them were sure one of them had killed another one of them.

Poker is one of those microcosms of life where the way one lives one's life becomes apparent. We had a giant poker game in Korea, one of those games that goes on and on until the people sitting at the table are three or four generations down the line from the people who originally started the game, and there's fifteen or twenty people's money circulating around the table; one or another goes broke, and one or another sits down and adds his wealth to the pot at the table, until it becomes a pretty impressive amount of money being circulated.

Unofficially, it had been like a poker tournament; the winners of the smaller games went up to play in the bigger games with the money they had won. The game had quite efficiently vacuumed up all the money in the company, and from farther abroad than that, until there was maybe twenty-five or thirty thousand dollars floating in the pot.

A poker game of that size draws attention; the tent was full of marines from my company and other nearby companies standing watching this game—that kind of money had a certain amount of drama to it. One of the guys watching grabbed another spectator by the shoulder, dragged him out of the tent and took him off behind a tree. He explained that he was kind of a card shark, and he could read marked cards, and that the deck of cards in use in this game was marked. From the way the flow of the game was going, he could tell who had introduced the marked deck: the big winner, with most of the company's filtered-down-through-the-tournament money sitting in front of him.

It was an example of an unofficial consensus; they got enough people from the company until some of them figured out what to do. The guy who could read the cards offered to go sit in the game and get the money back. So a few people got a little money together so he'd have a stake, and we sent him in to sit in on the game.

The tide began to change, slowly at first and then faster and faster until it was a torrent of money racing across the table from one side to the other. The guy who had introduced the marked deck of cards was beginning to look sicker and sicker; he was beginning to realize that somebody had it made. Being in a card game with someone who has a marked deck is a hard way to go; but being in a card game with a marked deck and having someone else in the game know how to read it, too, with fifty or sixty hostile witnesses standing around, is a pretty hard way to go, too.

The head winner, a guy none of us recognized from another company, offered to get up and leave. He said he was about even with how he had come into the game; but he still had quite a lot of money sitting in front of him. Everybody said, "No, the game ain't over yet."

The cards continued to be dealt and played, although by that time there was no longer any question of which way the flow of the money was going. It was no longer a sporting event, and everybody knew it.

He threw down his cards when he lost his last hand, and said he was broke. Three or four of the guys wanted to take him out behind the tent and rough him up a little; but the rest of the guys said, "No, no, leave him alone. He's sick enough as it is."

We let him go, and he went off down to wherever he came from. We looked at our new champion and asked him, what about the money. He said,

"I don't feel right about this money, because it was cheated back down the line and it ain't really my money. We have to figure out what to do with...It's *almost* enough to throw a beer bust for the regiment."

Tiny Kerrigan, a lieutenant who was rumored to own *blocks* of office space in San Francisco, said, "I'll match the pot. Then there'll be enough to throw a beer bust for the regiment."

They got all the cash together. Tiny, being an officer, had the power to make a few moves. I think he might have been in on ordering up the beer from Inchon. A United States boat full of beer. Nothing too good for our troops. Carling's Red Cap, Schlitz, Pabst, Bud, the works.

We went down with a fleet of trucks and purchased five thousand cases of beer. We decided to throw a beer bust for the Fifth Marine Regiment, who was going on line. We scheduled the beer bust for the day before we were going to leave for the combat zone.

Our company was the host. We went to prepare the area, and we found a large rice paddy that was dry. We sent out people to scavenge what we could find among the equipment and rubbish of the Army and the Marine Corps. They came back with two-by-twelves ten feet long, fifty-five gallon drums, and pontoons from pontoon bridges. We built a bar of two-by-twelves on oil drums, a hundred yards long; behind it, we set up the pontoons, great blunt-ended skiffs twenty-five feet long, eight or ten feet wide, loaded full of ice, brought in on six-by-six trucks. Then came the beer caravan, army six-by trucks loaded level-full with beer.

There was a great cheer, and we began unloading the beer, cracking cases of beer on the edges of the pontoons like eggs, and spilling the cans down into the ice. We loaded up the beer into the ice, and got ready for the party. We strung a few flags from the bar, and began the serious business of having a beer party.

Rabelais would have loved it. We situated the urinals over the hill and into a small hollow barely out of sight of the bar. We sank a few shell casings into holes full of gravel. It was woefully inadequate. Within hours they were full, and the hollow was full twenty feet across and three feet deep, a foaming yellow lake surrounded by marines. We filled a five acre field ankle deep in beer cans, and drank so much beer that everybody forgot about where they were going and sang Irish songs and Italian songs and Jewish songs and got drunk and fought and fell down in the dirt and threw up.

We began a more friendly poker game, not a big-money game, but one where the table consisted of stacked cases of beer and the chairs were more stacked cases of beer and we played and drank until we were sitting on the floor and playing on the floor.

On the morning after the regimental beer party, Able Company, Fifth Marine Regiment, fell out for inspection to go on line. It was amazing how every Marine there, from the privates to the corporals to the captains was able to fall out a perfectly turned out, sharp company of Marines, without anyone mentioning the fact that every regulation pack included an entire case of beer. We went on line with a case per man.

There is an honest way to play poker. Not sentimental, but honest.

Hill Ninety

Hill Ninety has always been symbolic of Korea to me, because it had the kind of insanity in it that truly typified the Korean War. Our company's area lay across the Panmunjom peace corridor, a road that stretched from South Korea to North Korea across No Man's Land, which was about three miles wide at that point. By agreement between the United Nations peacekeeping forces and the Republic of North Korea, it was agreed that no one would fire into a corridor four hundred meters wide surrounding that road, and that no one would fire across it except with high altitude fire like rocket fire or mortar fire, but no direct fire across it, and that it would be open for the crossing of diplomats.

In order to keep Panmunjom from being accidentally bombed during air strikes, on the site of the council grounds, which were on the thirty-eighth parallel, there was a large searchlight which pointed up in the sky all night, to keep the airplanes away. Our company area lapped across the entire peace corridor. I could sit on top of my bunker in a white t-shirt in the sun, and clean my rifle and watch the war go on a few hundred meters down the hillside. No one would fire into our area or fire out.

Hill Ninety was about in the middle of No Man's Land between our fortified post, Hill Two-Twenty-Nine, and the Chinese side, Three Fingers, Horseshoe. Hill Ninety—ninety meters high—had one long finger which stretched down into the actual peace corridor, about halfway across. Therefore,

Hill Ninety was mentioned in the agreement that established the thirty-eighth parallel, and it was said that we would defend it with only one rifle squad, and that they would not take it; they would not attack it because of its proximity to the corridor, and the danger of its slopping over into the corridor.

We put a rifle squad on Hill Ninety, and the Chinese promptly took it, captured the hill. We sent out a·massive probe, and retook the hill. Then, according to the agreement, we restaffed it with one rifle squad.

The reoccupation of Hill Ninety demonstrates the operations in the grey area between diplomacy and, as von Clausewitz assures us, the next step, which is war. Hill Ninety was established as a one-rifle-squad-defended hill, with one rifle squad, reinforced with a machine gun section with seven thirty caliber machine guns; a mortar section with five sixty millimeter mortars; two tanks and a quad fifty on a half-track. When I did my time on Hill Ninety, it was as a member of a reinforced rifle squad.

On top of our outpost, there were bunkers for two Long Tom fifty caliber machine guns, air-cooled with barrels nearly six feet long, with a cartridge longer than your hand, and a slug a half inch thick, armor-piercing incendiary tracers, bright, fluorescent red like a highway flare.

In front of the bunker was a line of trench, with a fighting hole on each side, where riflemen or light automatic weapons could defend in the case of close action. The little hilltop and the low brush of the hill looked like New Mexico; but the resemblance ended with the rice paddies at the foot of the hill.

Far across the paddies on the other side of No Man's Land, was a matching bunker with a Maxim fifty-one caliber machine gun, a huge, World War II relic like our Long Tom fifty, that rolled into its North Korean bunker on iron wheels forged in Europe.

One night in the dark of night, with a flare or a mortar flash going off somewhere up and down the five miles visible from our outpost, the Maxim opened up in the direction of one of our Long Tom 50's. We saw green communist tracers probing into the top of our hill, crashing through the brush and into the rocks; then the crew of the fifty returned the fire, and opened up an all night duel. Maybe as much as a mile or two of line shut down, and all eyes watched the red and green tracers float lazily back and forth across the eight hundred or a thousand yards between the bunkers. I don't think anyone expected any of them to ever hit; it was more like fireworks.

I would stick my head out of the fighting hole while the fifty fired, watch the red tracers float across the valley under the bright/dark starry sky, and when I saw the muzzle flash of the Maxim, I would duck down into the bottom of the fighting hole and stay there until I heard the Maxim's shells explode against our hill; then I would poke my head back out to see our Long Tom fifty's answer.

When you're fired on with a machine gun, it doesn't come at you orderly. It's like Mark Twain said about a cavalry charge: he said a cavalry charge is like throwing a handful of gravel at a barn door. A couple hit, then a big bunch of them, then a couple more.

I saw what Hill Ninety could be one night, walking across a dried up rice paddy bed at the base of the hill. The man in front of me hit a trip wire and set off a flare, a giant magnesium white light that lit up a half-mile circle bright as daylight, hanging on a parachute, hanging there for minutes. We stood frozen, knowing that any move we made would be seen in that bright light.

That night there was fire from the top of Hill Ninety towards the other side of the line. They were firing all the mortars and, at one point, they opened up right over our heads with the quad fifty with tracers. A five foot square river of fire running overhead with a sound like a freight train, two thousand rounds a minute. Rocket ripples fired from behind our backs—little trails of sparks went over our head and suddenly a whole quarter of the skyline erupted in white light and piercing white smokes of white phosphorus.

Fire fight, it turned out. We traveled out through the side

gate, across the line, across the break through the minefields, following a river of communications wire, each wire a sixteenth of an inch in diameter, but a broad path about four feet wide and a couple of inches deep; each patrol that went out carried a sound telephone, and each patrol strung a new wire, not trusting any of the previous wires to not be tapped by the enemy.

As we got farther out onto No Man's Land, there was a shot which struck a rock between me and the fellow in front of me. I was at the rear point of the patrol. Sparks were struck where the bullet hit, and shots erupted from the top of Hill Ninety.

We all lay down and, almost as one, the whole patrol rolled over on their side, unbuttoned their pants, and urinated in the rice paddy.

I remember running fast toward the hill where the fire fight was, mortar shells landing in the paddies so close that the water came down over me. Stopping by a low, run down, dirt, adobe and rock wall from an old Korean dwelling, waiting for a break in the fire to go over the top of the wall, I listened to the incoming. You learn the pitch and the tune and the song of every shell. I heard an incoming Korean 123 millimeter mortar, and the tune it played said it was for me. If it's going to go over you, the pitch rises; if it's going to drop short of you, the pitch falls; but if it's going to come at you, the pitch stays constant and just gets louder.

The pitch stayed constant and just got louder and louder until I thought it was going to land right on top of me. There was a large crash in the paddy nearby. It didn't go off. A guy says,

"What's that?"

I said, "I don't know if it's a dud or a delayed action." We were still under a bit of fire, and we weren't too hot to go over the top of the wall.

In one of those crazy things that you do, which I have done a couple of times before in my life, I crawled over to the shellhole and tried to find the shell so I could listen to it and see if it was ticking, to see if it was a delayed action.

The fire backed off and they told me to come over the wall. I jumped over the wall and went on up the hill.

I ran into the first wounded coming back down the hill, and it became completely irrelevant to carry a weapon. I carried stretcher when I could. I wasn't very strong. I carried other people's guns for them. I lost my gun. I left my ammunition belt lying around and a tank ran over it.

When we were bringing the wounded back, I tried to carry the stretcher with Red Grey, a small redhead who enjoyed having two colors for a name. He had been hit about an inch on either side of his backbone by burp gun fire. Burp guns were cheap sheet metal machine guns with a very high rate of fire that had been supplied by the Chinese communists. I tried to carry the stretcher, but my vision was so bad I couldn't avoid the bumps, and kept joggling him. Every joggle, he would scream. I turned it over to someone else I thought might do better, but they didn't do much better. I walked beside the stretcher with several rifles on my shoulder—the stretcher bearers'—and held Red's hand, and begged him,

"Please be quiet. Don't scream like that. Don't call down another patrol on us. If you make noise, you're liable to attract them. They're liable to see us. They're liable to fire on us, and we won't be able to get you out of here. You gotta shut up, so we can get you out of here. Come on, Red, please shut up."

I held his hand, and carried him back to the rear. I saw him disappear into a big, green armored personnel carrier along with a lot of other wounded guys. I heard he died, and then again I met someone I was in the Marine Corps with years and years later and he told me Red Grey didn't die at all. I'd thought he was dead all those years, and I was real glad to know he was living.

I took off the coat of my uniform and gave it to a guy who was wounded, shivering and shaking in shock. After he had disappeared into the inside of the armored personnel carrier, I remembered, *My glasses. They're in the pocket of the shirt I gave the guy. I've got to climb inside there and get them.*

I climbed down inside. They had a dim red light on, like the light in a photographic darkroom, that wouldn't show outside the armored personnel carrier and draw any fire. It was a small, steel room full of men screaming and moaning and bleeding. I had to scruffle around in the pile and move a couple over who screamed at me for moving them. I didn't dare lose my glasses; it was my last pair, and I couldn't be without glasses on line.

I found my shirt and got my glasses out, and climbed back out of the inside of the personnel carrier. If Dante had ever been inside one of those, he would have had a name for which exact level of hell it was.

Later that night we were asked for volunteers to go back out on patrol and bring in bodies. Me and Flanagan and a bunch of guys from the First Platoon went out. There was one guy there, a real decent corporal who was our squad leader. We went out and we found bodies, and they were chilled, stiff and cold, and there was no convenient way to carry them. The squad leader hefted one up on his shoulder, which stuck into the side of the hip, and carried him on his shoulder like a two-by-four, stuck out straight and stiff on both sides, back to camp.

We kept talking on the radio back to the base, that we have found more bodies and here we come. We came back and we found willing hands at the bottom of the hill to take the body we were carrying, and carry it back up the hill. I don't remember who that body was. But I remember several of the guys who died that night.

Corporal Miller, of the Buffalo Shuffle. Corporal Miller was a decent guy, and there were guys who wondered what he was doing in the service. He was from Buffalo, and when people would talk back he would say,

"If you get after me I'll do the Buffalo Shuffle on you."

He would hoist up his dukes like he was going to fight and shuffle comically sideways and say,

"Better not mess with the Buffalo Shuffle."

But that night on the hill, he lay on the ground wrestling with a stretcher. In a fit of frustration, he stood up and kicked the supports on the stretcher to open it up. As he did, a machine gun took off the top of his head. He fell back to the ground and someone else carried the stretcher.

Weeks later, going to the chow hall, we walked across an area where a bunch of gear was stored, and I never really knew if it was true, but guy pointed out a helmet with a mess in it and said it was Miller's helmet and the top of Miller's head.

Another fellow was killed who must have had a presentiment of death. In our last big beer bust before we went on line, he had become so drunk and so crazy, screaming and hollering and tearing at people, that they gave him a shotglass of paraldehyde. They didn't know for sure what it was that drove him wild. But he was dead within a week on line anyway.

After the firefight on Hill Ninety, I watched Corporal Cannon sit and cry about all the men that were lost. I tried to feel a way to do the same kind of grief he was doing and I couldn't find a way to do that kind of grief. I didn't know how to be. Later on I went down in my bunker, eight feet by eight feet underground, and continued to try to speak about the deaths of all those guys who died by Hill Ninety and the rice paddy. I was given the secret teaching by Labriola, a draftee from New York, who said,

"Shut up."

And it was a relief to shut up.

I'll never forget the only guy I ever saw who refused to go out on patrol. We were in awe of him. It was like he was something special, something we didn't know what to do about. They asked him to go on patrol and he said,

"No."

They said, "Why not," and he said,

"Because I'm afraid I'll get killed."

They said, "But you take the same risks as anybody else."

"I'm not going. I'm afraid I'll get killed."

We all stood around and looked at him like he was Superman, like he was magic. It was weird. We kept waiting to see what would happen to him. Were they going to tie him to a tree and shoot him? What were they going to do? What do you do?

We all watched him very closely, and they never let us find out what happened. They just transferred him away to the rear and we never knew what happened to him. We never knew what happened to the one that took a life, and we never knew what happened to the one who wouldn't go.

Is That You, Love?

One of the things about pacifism is having a realistic idea about what it is that you can do. I see on television all these Kung Fu and Bionic Man one-punching everybody, slipping in these fast punches that nobody ever comes back from, and I always think that's misleading. One of the things I saw in the Marine Corps is what it's like when some big strong men fight.

We were in twelve weeks of boot camp in those days. When they lined us up to march, they wanted the platoon to look nice and neat and tidy—the Marine Corps *loves* it to look nice and neat and tidy—so the men were all lined up in order of height. The first four across the front were all the six-footers, and on down the line. From a certain perspective, they all looked like they were the same size. The drill instructors were all pretty insulting to the men at the rear of the lines, and called them the feather merchants. Because of the weirdities of genetics and the excessive amounts of cow's milk I drank in my youth, I turned out four inches taller than my father and eight inches taller than my mother; so I was in the front four, six feet tall and a hundred and sixteen pounds. Next to me were Love and Sims, and another professional soldier who had signed on to the Marine Corps for his second hitch after doing his first hitch in the army.

Sims was from Oklahoma, with a bright fiery red face. Love was black. They were probably six-two or three apiece, probably over two hundred pounds each. In the morning that we were lined up the first day, the drill instructor stepped out

37

in front of the company, looked at the front four, and told
Love he was the Right Guide, the secondary commander of
the platoon. He would march on the right front flank, and
the platoon would take orders from him, under orders from
the drill instructor.

"Love," the drill instructor said, "Can you whip everybody
in this platoon?"

Love said, "Sir, I don't know every man in this platoon."

"Well, you fall out and take a look at them," the D.I. said.

Love stepped out of line and walked back to the end of the
line, back by the feather merchants, and he looked them
over. He looked at each man as he walked up the line,
walking faster past the feather merchants, but slowing down
as he came up to the bigger men in front. He came up to
where the first four were, dismissing me with a glance,
looking a bit more carefully at the ex-doggie, and finally
stopping by Sims from Oklahoma, and walking completely
around him twice, looking him up and down.

He stepped back into line, snapped back to attention,
looked at the drill instructor, and said,

"Yes, sir."

I had heard Love talk, and had seen him move, and I
thought that was all right. He seemed like a pretty good
dude, gentle and black, big, quiet. But that night, I heard a
disturbance behind our Quonset hut, and got up to go out
and see what was happening.

Sims could not stand to take orders from a black man.
Love and Sims were fighting to see if Love was going to be
the Right Guide of the platoon, or if Sims was. They stood in
a circle, and without science or beauty or much grace, swung
and hit each other in the chest and the face with great
smacking whacks that sounded like slapping on a side of
beef, with grunts and groans; they beat on each other until it
became less a question of who was going to knock whom
down than of who was going to be left standing.

Sims finally absorbed so many punches that his legs
began to crumple, and he fell. I was glad Love had won. I
was a little afraid of Sims.

At roll call in the morning, it was obvious that something had happened during the night; Love and Sims both looked bad.

The drill instructor walked up to Love.

"Love?"

"Yessir."

"Are you still Right Guide?"

"Yessir."

I'll never forget Love's voice. Years later, after boot camp and thirteen months as a brig guard at the military prison at Camp Pendleton, walking up a dark road in Korea in the middle of the night, I was suddenly challenged by a sentry out of my sight who said,

"Halt! Who goes there?"

I thought, *I've heard that sweet, thick, black voice before.* I said, "Is that you, Love?"

Love said, "Who-o is that out there?"

I said, "It's me, man, don't you know me?"

I came up, and sure enough, it was Love. I knew I could recognize his voice anywhere.

Farts and Mother H

Able Company, First Battalion, Fifth Marine Regiment, had several company corpsmen, but far and away the most memorable were Farts and Mother H.

Farts' claim to immortality lay in his ability to produce as many as forty-two separate and distinct explosions, earning him his honorific. Farts had a certain style as a corpsman. If you were hurt, he was like one of the other guys on the football team—compassionate, but a little rough.

Farts was short and round, and seemed well-built for his specialty. Mother H. was tall and handsome, with close-cut black, curly hair, a fine-looking young man who wanted nothing more than to resume his homosexual life in San Francisco. Our platoon felt special about having a gay corpsman. We felt we got better treatment. Mother H. was kind and compassionate. We felt we were being cared for. Mother H. obviously loved us, and felt tender and gentle impulses which were appreciated in combat. We were an integrated platoon. Our corpsman loved us, and we loved our corpsman.

Occasionally I saw a corpsman make a silly mistake. Once they began looking at a growth, a small wart or excrescence on somebody's stomach, and decided they wanted to open it up and see more inside it. They sprayed it with ethyl chloride to freeze it, and got out a scalpel and began cutting on it, without noticing that the patient was standing up, and was beginning to turn pale green, swaying gently to and fro, about to fall over while they were still intent on the bright circle of white light with the red center, and the flashing blades of the scalpels.

Mother was good on patrols. We went out not long after full dark, out the Panmunjom peace corridor, past the red and white candy-striped guard shacks, with the spiffy guard in his white gloves, white spats and white duty belt, chrome helmet, and turned off the peace corridor towards Three Fingers and Horseshoe, Chinese-held hills. We managed to penetrate fairly deeply into Chinese territory without alerting any sentries or guards, and turned and came back towards our own lines, looking for the sally gate where we could re-enter our own trenches.

There was a trench line drawn all the way across Korea, roughly at the thirty-eighth parallel. A row of trench, machine gun bunkers and fighting holes spaced every few yards, a row of twenty- or thirty-foot wide tanglefoot barbed wire five feet deep with barbed wire in loose tangles, *rolls* of it, mined with occasional trip flares. Outside the row of barbed wire was our mine field. The mine field, for the safety of the U.N. peacekeeping forces, had one strand of barbed wire fence running down the side of the mine field next to the trench line, with a small, red triangle hanging every few feet, and on the post a sign: *Warning! Mine Field.*

As we approached the sally gate, the patrol ran up against the barbed wire fence, saw the red triangles, found the sign. We leaned over and peered at the sign in the darkness, and found that we were reading the sign upside down. It was facing the other way. We were standing in the mine field. We had crossed the mine field, and had now come to the edge of it.

We started to step over the fence and continue when the sergeant in charge of the patrol said,

"No. We made it this far. We're going to turn around and retrace our steps through the mine field, go back and re-enter through the peace corridor."

Opinions flared, whether to cross over the fence and go back, or to retrace our steps back through the mine field, when suddenly Mother H. drew his .45, kicked back the slide, and pointed it at the sergeant.

"Sergeant," he said, "This appears to me to be a health question. I'm in charge of health, and it looks unhealthy to retrace our steps back across that minefield after we were lucky enough to make it the first time. We're going to step over the fence, and go in through our sally port. And if you want to run me up when we get back to company area, you can; but that's what we're going to do now."

The sergeant looked down the barrel of a .45, which is a pretty big barrel anyway, and looks *real* big when it's pointed at you. He agreed, and we stepped over the strand of barbed wire, walked down and found the sally port, re-entered our own trench lines, and got back to our company area.

We waited to see what was going to happen to Mother H. Some of us feared for his safety; it could be called mutiny. There were dark rumors that people who did things wrong in combat situations were stood up against the wall and shot.

The next day, while we waited, Mother H. and the sergeant told their story to the Captain. Mother H. came back down to the tent, and we all asked,

"What happened to you? What happened to you?"

"Nothing happened to me. And the sergeant is relieved of duty as a squad leader, and sent to the rear to be a cook."

That was one of the few good-sense decisions I saw come down through the official channels of the Marine Corps. But we thought, "Mother H. takes good care of us."

The Occupation

After the war was over, our company stayed on line, covering the same area of line across the Panmunjom peace corridor that we had covered during wartime; but now we were part of the guards of the Demilitarized Zone, which stretched from Hill Two-Twenty-Nine on across No Man's Land.

The tension in our camp after the war was different than the tension during the war. Crazy things happened. We went out on several patrols a night. I climbed over Hill Two-Twenty-Nine from end to end in the middle of the night so many times that it became like an amusement park ride: so many steps up the hill, jump over the rock, down the shale slide, pull yourself up on the barbed wire, up the next hill, stop at the top, talking back on radios, radio check from the top of Hill Two-Twenty-Nine, and back into camp.

Camp was just back off the line, just on the back side of Hill Two-Twenty-Nine. It was a funny place, a tent camp of sixteen-by-thirty-two-foot squad tents, eight or nine of them in a row. They brought in wood, and told us we could build floors in the tents. We were delighted; we'd been on dirt and rock floors for so long. We found out the floors were not just for cleanliness; but our camp was also considered expendable in case of a Red Chinese attack, which we referred to by the term, "In case Luke should jump off," short for Luke the Gook.

Our life was measured and dealt in terms of whether Luke

would jump off or not. The camp was designed to self-destruct if we had to leave. The floors of the tents were sprayed with kerosene so they could just have a match touched to them. We had a fuel dump which contained the heating oil that kept the iron stoves going in the wintertime—thirty or fifty fifty-five gallon drums of stove oil. I noticed that one of the drums seemed to be different than the others; one end was painted white. I asked why that drum seemed special.

The sergeant in charge of the fuel dump pointed up to the brow of a hill, where a fifty-caliber machine gun sat in a bunker. He said,

"That fifty-caliber machine gun up there on that hill is aimed at that white barrel. That white barrel is not full of stove oil like the other barrels; it's full of gasoline. And the fifty-caliber is loaded with tracers. It's designed so that the guy up in that bunker can set the whole camp on fire in one flash."

Living in a self-destruct area took its toll. We averaged a crackup rate of about two per cent a month, people who would just wig and scream, and have to be carried away, fighting.

Tensions had mounted to the point where it was time for another beer bust, about the only thing we were allowed to do to let it out. We had a beer ration, and by this time, although only nineteen years old, I was old in the ways of the Marine Corps. I was a fire team leader, and several men in my fire team didn't drink, so I had several people's beer rations to dispose of every day.

We ordered up a bunch of beer, and iced it up in a jeep trailer full of ice. We parked the trailer in the basketball court, and began drinking beer, talking earnestly and closely, head to head, drinking beer, trying to talk about something besides Korea. Our squad leader, a corporal from the midwest, was one of the most honest people I ever saw in the Marine Corps, one of the few of us who seemed to be some kind of a grownup, the only one I ever heard of who went to Japan and actually bought gifts for his wife and family, and didn't sleep with the prostitutes. He was so honest we almost couldn't believe him. He was the guy who carried the stiff bodies with us on Hill 90.

It became a challenge to try to get him to drink some beer. We got him to drink a beer, and he got a little giggle on. We got him to drink a couple more beers, and he got a little bit of a laugh on, and got to saying,

"Hey, this beer ain't so bad. It feels pretty good." He was having a good time, when the beer bust began to get to that fever pitch where somebody said,

"Hey! Let's throw the gunny in the ice trailer."

Several men ran up to our company gunnery sergeant, an old veteran of many wars, eighty-four months overseas in combat zones in various wars for the United States Marine Corps, and dunked him in the ice trailer.

They said, "Let's dunk the topkick in the ice trailer!"

And we dunked the topkick in the ice trailer. Then we dunked the lieutenant, and the first lieutenant, and even the captain. We were high and giddy when we dunked the captain in the ice trailer. It felt fine to dunk the captain in the ice trailer.

Then we stood around looking at each other with all that energy. Over underneath the basketball hoop, a fight broke out. Several men walked over to the fight to break it up, and each combatant was grabbed from the rear by a well-wisher who dragged him back; and each combatant promptly turned and began to fight with the well-wisher who, drunk and angered at being unjustly assaulted when just trying to keep him out of trouble, began to swing back. Each of those pairs of combatants were dragged apart by four more, who were then drawn into the fight. The entire two hundred fifty men led into a riot, just like the old atomic energy demonstration where they throw the ping pong ball in on top of all the mousetraps. They all stood there and fought and slugged it out, except for two: me, who didn't like fighting and was not husky enough to participate; and, up on a hill sitting in front of the tent, the corporal, our squad leader, crying and crying and crying, wishing he wasn't drunk and hating to see everyone fight, sick and sad and sorry.

I felt bad about us getting him drunk. It almost broke his heart.

We were a mixed bag of draftees and enlistees, and many of us saw folks from other parts of the country for the first time. Zanalini and Labriola told us about the city, the Big Apple. One young round fellow lost his original name and was nicknamed "The Gunch", sometimes known as "The Scrunchin' Gunch".

We spent many long nights together with no social life but one another, hanging out. Sometimes I would get the ingredients together and make hot chocolate for the squad. Sometimes we would drink beer. Sometimes someone would get some special food from home, and we would cook it up on our oil stove. We gave each other backrubs, and told each other the stories of our lives.

It was customary, for the noncommissioned officers at least, to hire Koreans to do their laundry. Everybody spoke a little bit of pidgin Korean—*skoshi* meant "not very much", as in *"skoshi time"*. *Taksan* was "a lot." *Ichiban*, Japanese for "Number One", meant "good". And *washy-washy* meant, "Would you do my laundry?"

The Marines had a casual contempt for the entire Korean nation, as tall, well-fed Americans do for shorter, darker, hungrier people. They said the main movie playing in Korea was Marilyn Monroe, Joe Louis and Syngman Rhee in "Screw, Fight, or Washy-Washy".

These same NCOs, I found one night when I went up to see a staff sergeant of my acquaintance, had engaged a Korean houseboy. They had him dressed up like a girl, and made up with lipstick and rouge. They had him dancing in the NCO tent. I was a little shocked to see that. In fact, although many people in the camp said they were surprised later on, I didn't feel surprised at all when it turned out that someone had slit the side of the noncommissioned officers' tent with a knife in a long cut, and had reached through that cut and taken weapons, cameras, and had robbed those NCOs. They thought it was a terrorist, but I just thought it was the guy they had made dress up like a girl and dance for them.

One night when the beer and the backrubs were mixed, a strange vibration came through our tent.

There was a little jealousy about who was going to rub the guy from Michigan's back, the one who confessed in his life story to wearing white bucks back at Michigan State, and being a frat rat.

As we stood in a circle drinking beer, with our arms around one another's shoulders, the boy from Michigan began to go to sleep. The fellow next to him, with his arms around his shoulders, would shake him and say, "Wake up! Wake up! Don't be a gunch!"

The guy on the other side would put his arm around him and pull him over to him and say,

"Leave him alone. Don't call him a gunch."

"He's worse than a gunch. He's a scrunching gunch."

There was something not quite right between Zanalini and the boy he called the gunch. Sometimes he was solicitous and kind and cared about him. And sometimes he just seemed to want to dominate him. Zanalini wanted to be friends, and gave him a lot of attention; but it often took the form of needling, sometimes very rough and insistent. The relationship continued until we went out to an outpost far out in miles from the company area, out in a rice paddy in a tent. There was little to do on the outpost but drink beer. We carried out packboards full of it. One time we went back for beer ration and came out, four of us, each carrying four cases of beer on a packboard, twenty-six pounds of beer a case, each one of us carrying a hundred and four pounds of beer. Halfway to the outpost, we tired. We sat down and tried to drink enough of the beer to lighten our load.

I guess we succeeded, because we made it the rest of the way to the outpost; but I fell off the dike in the paddy, and wasn't sober enough to climb back on the dike. Then I fell on my hands and knees and wasn't sober enough to stand up. I crawled on my hands and knees across a paddy eighteen inches deep in muddy water, cresting the mud like an Irish setter coming in with a duck in its mouth. I crawled on my hands and knees up out of the paddy and into our tent. I collapsed on the floor and felt hands fumbling with the straps of my pack. Then I realized that it was not help. They had no intention of picking me up. They were just opening the top case so they could get some beer out. I lay on the floor for a while until I could get up enough strength to climb out from under the cases of beer.

Those cans, when empty, were thrown in the paddy, along with many more, including a great thirty-case beer bust, until an officer came to inspect our outpost and found that we were in the middle of a circle of beer cans with a radius as far as a beer can could be thrown, full of beer cans every couple of feet. The officer was livid:

"Get those cans out of that paddy!"

It was a perfect example of subconscious. We had never seen the beer cans until they were drawn to our attention.

The officer required us to get those cans out of there, get some rocks up and build some flower beds around the front of the tent, put some white rocks around the edge of the flower bed, and get this thing looking a little company area around here. So the Gunch and Zanalini and I went out to dig a hole about six feet by six feet by six feet to bury all the beer cans in.

I was in the bottom of the hole with an entrenching tool when Zanalini's constant needling of the gunch pushed me to the point where I climbed screaming up out of the hole, waving the entrenching tool. I grabbed Zanalini by the collar and told him,

"Leave him alone. I can't stand to listen to anybody get picked on so much. Don't pick on him any more. Leave him alone, or I'm going to hit you with this here shovel!"

Zanalini looked in my eyes and saw that I was seriously overwrought, and backed it down.

One day, through some level of magic which I did not understand, someone from the rear came up and gave us a case of DeKuyper Sloe Gin. It was a thick, red, syrupy drink. I actually drank a fifth of it. I got seriously drunk, and staggered out of the tent to stand and pee at the edge of the paddy, and fell down the paddy dike into the water. I thrashed around until at least my head was up, and I lay in the freezing cold water so long that the ice began to form around the edge of my fatigues, too drunk to stand up, still carrying a half-empty bottle of sloe gin I'd carried out in case I wanted another drink before I came back.

As I looked up, a large silhouette blacked the sky directly above my head, and I looked up to see a Marine fumbling with his pants buttons, about to pee on my head.

"Wait, man, wait a minute. I'm down here."

"Who's that?"

"It's just me here in the paddy, man."

"Hey, what you got?"

"A bottle of sloe gin."

He stepped down and took my bottle of sloe gin and went back inside the tent and didn't even pick me up out of the paddy. But at least he got me mad enough that I got enough gumption to crawl back out of the paddy by myself and crawl back in and pass out inside the tent.

I had been in Korea long enough to have an idea how the ropes worked. I felt like taking a little walk; I needed to be alone by myself for a while. I thought, *Well, I've got a couple of pairs of glasses; I'll just stash one pair in my sea bag out of sight, and take the other one and knock a lens out. Then I can go up to the company's first sergeant, and ask him if I can go back to the MASH unit and get my glasses replaced.* This is not an impulse I am particularly proud of; but I think it is one that most people who were in the low ranks of the military will recognize.

I started off towards the rear. Walking down the road, rifle over my shoulder, I didn't think of myself as being armed, although I had a clip of ammunition with me. I was enjoying one of the few freedoms we had in Korea, to walk along a dirt road and look at some strange scenery for a few miles. My first adventure on the road.

I saw a couple of jeeps coming my way. I was deep in my head, and didn't want to talk to anybody. I figured anybody in a jeep was probably an officer anyway. I didn't want to look at any officers. I didn't want to have to salute anybody. I didn't want to be bothered with anybody from the upper classes of the military. So I waited until just before they were going to appear around the corner onto the stretch of road where I was. I dropped down on one knee, untied my boot, and tied my boot with my head down as the entire caravan drove by. It turned out to be four or five jeeps. I never looked up, tied my boot and continued on down to the MASH unit.

It was a nice, hot summer day. The sunshine was bright. I found my way through the tents of the military hospital unit, Baker med. I stepped into the tent where I was directed to check in, into a shadow so dim as to seem almost completely dark after the bright sunshine outside. The floor was rough wooden planks laying in the dirt. I looked up at the corpsman and went completely dizzy, and passed out, falling flat on my face in the middle of the floor. I woke up on a stretcher listening to myself talking, babbling.

"You got to get me off line. I been on line for months and months and months. I been on line too long. You got to get me out."

I heard what I was saying and closed my mouth, shut up and sat up. The doctors were questioning me closely, with the idea that they might take me off line. I was still wondering how come I fainted when I ducked in the door, and was somewhat disturbed to have found myself babbling about something that had not been sitting in my forebrain, something that I did not know was a problem or a question or an issue in my brain until I heard myself babbling it to the corpsman.

I reversed all engines, told them everything was all right, just fine, said, "See you later on," and left.

I got outside and walked back to the company area as fast as I could, without mentioning anything about glasses. I got my other glasses out of my duffel bag, assuming the sergeant would think they were the glasses I went back to get, and tried to forget the whole thing.

As it turned out, I wasn't allowed to forget quite all of it. It turned out that the five jeeps that passed me had been my platoon commander, a lieutenant, whom I should have saluted; my company executive officer, a first lieutenant, whom I should have saluted; my company commander, a captain, whom I should have saluted; the regimental battalion commander, a light colonel, whom I should have saluted; the regimental commander, a full colonel, whom I also should have saluted. They were taking a general from the army on tour, whom I also should have saluted. The company sergeant, barely controlling the rage in his voice, said,

"Not everyone manages to avoid saluting his entire chain of command!"

One of my favorite pastimes was a little game I used to play over the question of saying "Sir". I didn't like to say "Sir". It wasn't as if people hadn't taught me since earliest youth that I was supposed to show respect; my mother used to hassle me and tell me I should say "Sir" to my Grandfather, which I only did after I was grown up. But I didn't like having to call an officer "Sir", possibly something about the question of being a gentleman by act of Congress. I have never been able to stand hierarchy.

I always felt that if you said something that was true enough and necessary enough, that you didn't have to go through any kinds of forms. I used to go stand close to a lieutenant or a captain and say quietly in his ear, in the soft and reasonable tone of voice of equals, things that had enough substance that he wouldn't notice I hadn't said "Sir"; and to develop this into a conversation where we began to speak as equals.

Some officers never understood I was doing this to them, and were just faintly troubled. But one lieutenant figured it out, and turned on me in the midst of a quiet and reasonable sentence, and snapped,

"You're supposed to call an officer 'Sir'."

Being caught like that blew me out in the open. It was two or three days before I could catch him off guard enough to do it to him again.

Cell Block Number Nine

When I came back from Korea, I was sent to Naval Air Station Alameda in Oakland, California, where I became a member of the Marine detachment of guards who guarded the gates and served as security for the Navy base where large naval ships, up to and including aircraft carriers, came in for change of crew and change of airplanes. The gate crew on the base was mostly comprised of fellows like myself who were just back from Korea and were going to get out in a few months. All of us had what you might call a short-timer's attitude. That is to say, we really didn't much care whether school kept or not. As well as the responsibility for the gate, within the Marine detachment was a smaller, somewhat more elite group called brig section, who took care of the small Marine Corps brig on the base. We were sort of stuck over on the edge of the airfield along with the other extra people on the base. Our barracks was next to the WAVEs' barracks, and many of us were friends with the WAVEs, and drank with the WAVEs in the enlisted man's club next door, which we referred to by its more informal name of the "Slop Chute."

One evening, my duty didn't come until late that night. I thought it probably wouldn't hurt anything, although I understood that it was frowned upon, for me to get down to Omar's Pizza Parlor in Oakland and have time for a pizza and a beer for supper, and get back well in time to go on duty. I had a couple of friends who were equally shiftless, and we decided to run out to Omar's and catch one. We had no trouble getting out the gate—all the gate crew were our friends.

Omar's was hot—lots of customers, a good atmosphere and a good attitude; and we ordered our pizza and sat down to drink a beer while our pizza was coming, when the bartender told me there was a phone call for me. Answering the telephone was one of those incautious moves that one learns to avoid with age. Sure enough, the voice on the other end of the phone was the Officer of the Day, a pretty good dude, not actually an officer, but a master sergeant who was taking his turn as Officer of the Day. His real interest in life was Tempest Storm, who danced the burlesque at the Del Rey Burlesque next door to the Jug Club on San Pablo. The Officer of the Day said on the phone,

"You got ten minutes to get back aboard this base."

My friends and I canceled our pizza order, ran out the back door, and jumped in the car, driving back to Alameda as fast as we could go, changing out of our Class A liberty uniforms into our dungarees as we came through the gate, and showing up as though we'd been on the base all the time, although the Officer of the Day had talked to me at Omar's Pizza Parlor on Telegraph. The Officer of the Day said,

"I'm going to lock you up until the Major comes back."

He sent me to the brig section, where I was given into the hands of the biggest man in the whole Marine detachment, a six-foot-six corporal who had a reputation as being rough in the brig detachment. I had special reason for wanting to avoid the corporal. He and I had been talking to the same WAVE at the Slop Chute, and there had been some discussion.

The Marine Corps is not the kind of organization where one is allowed to express one's opinions or ask what is going on. I merely had to obey the orders that were given to me; and the penalty for non-obedience to these orders was to receive yet more time in the brig under the corporal's power. I tried as hard as I could to do everything I was asked; I had no choice.

The first night wasn't so bad: mop the floor, polish the bars on the cells, polishing along on cell number nine while the radio sang the old rock and roll song, *Cell Block Number Nine:*

> *There's a riot going on,*
> *'Way down in Cell Block Number Nine.*

Even combing out the mop until every strand hung as straight as well-brushed hair, so the mop would be perfect, didn't seem too bad. But the morning was different. First, the corporal took me out and had my head shaved; then he had me perform calisthenics. First, toe touches until my back was fiery with fatigue. Then, on my back, sit-ups. I used to say I could do sit-ups indefinitely; I found out I couldn't do sit-ups indefinitely. After a few hundred, my stomach muscles were almost destroyed. Then to another exercise, standing up, bending from side to side, and I began to realize the corporal had a plan. He was systematically breaking down the muscles around my waist.

I dared not disobey. I continued. More push-ups. More sit-ups. More toe-touches. Faster and faster. "On your back." "On your belly." "On your feet." "On your back." "On your belly." "On your feet." "On your back." "On your belly." "On your feet."

I did hours and hours of calisthenics until all the muscles around my waist were so broken down, and fatigued, and sore, that I could only stand perfectly erect; if I bent over from the vertical the slightest amount, I either had to grab support with my hands, or fold over like a piece of wet laundry. I could not hold myself up.

When the corporal saw that I was broken down about as far as I could be broken down by using my own strength against me, he took me out into the narrow alley between the brig section's barracks and the WAVEs' barracks, opposite the window of the WAVE we had been speaking to in the Slop Chute, and told me that I had to repeat after him, and shout as loud as I could,

"My name is Spider Gaskin, and I am a shit bird, and my

heart pumps shit."

I was ordered to repeat that sentence again and again, on pain of more calisthenics, until my throat was so used up that it was obvious and apparent to the corporal that I could not yell—not that I *would not*, but that I *could not* yell any more.

The next morning, Monday morning, the Major came back aboard the base, and received word from the topkick that I was in the brig. He came out and gave me two weeks' restriction for having been off the base during duty time.

The Draft

On the way home from Korea we sang, to the tune of "Chattanooga Choo-Choo",

Pardon me boy,
Is that the Indochina convoy?
Uncle Sam has my fare
And just a trifle to spare
Leave that Yokohama Harbor about a quarter to four.
Sink a submarine and you're ready for more.
Dinner on the liner
Nothing could be finer
Than to have your ham and eggs in Indochina.

Back in World War II, the medics in the field didn't carry weapons. There was a set of agreements made between all the civilized countries of the world, called the Geneva Convention, and it was agreed there that medics wouldn't carry weapons, and that nobody would fire on them. Then we got into some real ugly race wars, where we hated the Japanese for being Japanese, and we hated the Germans for being German, and the Germans hated us for being Americans, and we all got into a lot of hate, and we began to pick off each other's ambulances. We began to shoot at each other's medics. Medics began to carry weapons.

By the time I got to Korea, when I was on line in combat, the medics all carried pistols. By Viet Nam, the medics all carried automatic weapons. In modern warfare, we had given up respect for the medics.

There is a young priest in Quiche province in Guatemala, where much of the violence has been going on. This young priest used to be in the Irish Republican Army, the I.R.A. He had gone and was being a priest up in the Quiche. He serves Mass. They have a picture in the newspaper of him with a wafer in his hand, with a little altar. He's radical, and he talks radical, and he has to sleep in a different place every night, because he knows there's a hit list out on him. Somebody wants him. Somebody wants to kill him. He has decided what kind of an example he's going to be to the Indians. He keeps a 357 magnum pistol under his Bible. He said the Archbishop of El Salvador was shot down at Mass. He says he's going to go down fighting; he thinks it's an example to the Indians for him to go down fighting.

That's really a tragic story. A dude with that kind of courage could set a better example. And the result of the example he sets is that it's open season on priests. They'll say,

"A priest might have a gun."

Every time civilization slips and loses that respect, all of mankind is a little less civilized. We've all slipped back toward the carnivores. I can't tell that priest to stay in Quiche and get killed any more than I could tell our PLENTY crew in Solola that they had to stay there when it was dangerous. But our guys were down there and they weren't carrying any guns. They were pretty safe not carrying any guns, because nobody was mad at them. They hadn't been trying to do anything wrong to the people. They hadn't been being rich gringos on the people, and they had been trying to help the people out. Even if they made mistakes, they were honest about it and tried to work it out.

I used to think it was a terrible mistake that I went in the Marine Corps. But I don't feel that way now. I want to be somebody who went to combat and carried weapons and was even a good shot, who didn't kill nobody, and ain't gonna, and don't wanna. I won't carry a gun. I'll carry the state of the art in radio, and whatever makes us fast and smart and able to move quickly—I'll go for all of that; but I don't want to carry anything for hurting some other people.

The archbishop said if he died it would be all right, because his spirit would rise again in the people.

It's hard not to take sides sometimes. That's what's tearing America up about the Middle East. It's hard on a left-wing Jew who finds himself cheering for the Jews against the PLO from being a Jew, and cheering for the PLO against the Jews from being a leftist. It's hard on them. They're just torn. Political ideals and family loyalty.

You have to rise above politics.

The arms race we're in now was built up between John Foster Dulles and Stalin, in great measure. When they asked Dr. Spock about pacifism, they asked him,

"Well, what could we have done about Korea? North Korea was going to jump off and take South Korea."

He said we could have noticed farther up the line that the South Korean regime was totalitarian and not worthy of our support, and not had anything to do with the whole thing. We wouldn't have separated Korea between us and Russia; we wouldn't have insisted on making it into two places and then fortifying them with two different armies. We created that hassle, and it didn't have to happen, because of the political actions that we took. We could have been *smarter* up the line, and *saved Korea*.

I'm forty-six now. I used to have that optimistic idea that there would be the war to end all wars—that everything would be so settled that you wouldn't have any wars any more. What I see now is the same kind of stuff that we slid into World War II with. The same kind of armies all over the world, in every country something revolutionary happening...

The draft has the deck so stacked against you that if you don't register, they turn you into a fugitive, and you have to go underground immediately. So you might as well go ahead and register, but write on your registration card that you are a conscientious objector and registering under protest, and refuse to sign a card that they won't let you write that on.

You get to say, the first time they get your name, they also get the information that you are a conscientious objector. That way, down the line, when it comes draft time and they come for you, you can say,

"I told you when I was eighteen and had to register that I was a conscientious objector. And I'm more mature in it now."

Make your stand there. If you make your stand against registration, it's a political football. But if you make your stand against going on the grounds that you're a conscientious objector and that you told them so the first time they ever asked you, that keeps you from having to go underground next week.

What if somebody came in and was going to take over your country and not let you practice your religion and arrest you for doing it? I was asked that by the Lions Club one time, and I had to remind them that someone had already come into my country (The Farm) and wouldn't let me practice my religion, and weren't they glad that we were non-violent?

If I see somebody going to do grievous bodily harm to somebody, I'd probably interfere, even at the cost of getting knocked on my can—it wouldn't be the first time.

But that question is very unfair. There's nobody on the continental United States, or on any territory that we really have any right to, who is doing anything like that. But we, on the other hand, are doing that to scores of other countries around the world.

So the question is not what we're going to do if someone comes to get us; it's more of what we're doing to other people.

The United States is not in any immediate danger. Other people are in danger from us.

By being non-violent, we're trying to reduce the probability of its happening. We're being actively non-violent. We're like anti-terrorists. In order to keep Latin America from invading the United States, we're trying to help out south of the border. And in order to help keep Africa from jumping off on the United States, well-deserved though it might be, we're over in Lesotho, over in that territory, doing something about it. If you're a pacifist, you act ahead of time, before the violence starts. If you're not a pacifist, you act when the violence starts.

Interlude

George Bernard Shaw made a serious lament in *Man and Superman*, when the devil pointed out that man really excels in the killing arts, and that most of the things we find from old cultures are weapons. But now a new level of fantasy has been reached.

On the newest computerized jet fighter bomber systems that the United States is building, the helmet is integral with the airplane, and is fastened to the top of the cockpit through a series of microswitches and servomotors. When the pilot inserts his head into this helmet and turns his head, every movement of his head and neck is translated into the aiming system. Fastened with a small holder to the side of the helmet is a small monocle with a crosshair. The plane has been designed to allow the pilot as much freedom to hunt as possible. The instruments are projected on the inside of the canopy, so the pilot just has to refocus from other airplanes or scanning the sky, back to the canopy to see what the instruments read. There is also a small microphone fastened to the helmet, which floats in front of the mouth. The pilot merely has to look at his target airplane, turn his head to follow its flight, line up the crosshairs on the monocle against the side of the other plane, and speak into his microphone any phrase he chooses, to send a Sidewinder infrared heat-seeking missile right straight up their exhaust pipe.

Even Zeus has to throw a thunderbolt; even Thor has to

throw his hammer; but mankind only needs to say, "Bang! You're dead."

Guns

I was raised with guns all my life. My father had guns; all my uncles had guns, on my father's side of the family. On my mother's side of the family, I suppose my great-grandfather, who was a prospector, probably had a gun.

I saw someone wrote just recently that there is a rite of passage about guns. Somewhere around twelve years old, they let you have a gun. I remember firing a heavy twelve gauge shotgun when I was about ten, which recoiled itself completely out of my grasp onto the ground when I fired it. When I was twelve, I got a .22 rifle; my father bought me a single shot. He said that automatic rifles are for poor shots. If you have a single shot rifle, you'll learn to be a better shot, because you have to make the first one count. I remember on many occasions firing on a running rabbit, and missing the first time, and never having a second chance. I'm not sure if my father's advice made me a better shot; but it saved the lives of many rabbits.

I only actually initiated one hunt on my own that was a successful hunt. It was not large, but the impact was sufficient. I was fourteen years old or so, living in Santa Fe, New Mexico, in the wintertime with six or eight inches of snow on the ground. I was home with the winter flu, and was wishing for something to do.

I glanced out the window and saw a large bluebird, sitting on top of the telephone pole fifty or sixty feet from the door of our house.

I picked up my BB gun, my trusty Daisy, cranked the lever, and stepped out the door briefly in my bathrobe and slippers. I carelessly threw the BB gun to my shoulder, and dropped the bluebird with one shot.

I was sick. I hadn't the slightest idea that I might hit him. I thought I might rattle the cables near him, drive him away or scare him, but my casual unthinking marksmanship was clean as Zen, and very deadly; it dropped the bluebird in the snow.

I walked out through the snow in my slippers and inspected him to see if he was really dead. I have never been able to fire on anything alive.

It is good to not be superstitious about guns, but to understand them, and to make your decisions from that place. I was raised with guns. In the Marine Corps, I became a medium good shot pretty quickly, because of my experience with guns as a youth: they were not anything strange to me. We were expected to try out with various kinds of weapons. I fired middle-grade sharpshooter with the M-1 rifle, the stock army rifle of the time, used through World War II, the Korean War and early Vietnam; but I had a knack with the automatic weapons. I fired high grades, expert, with the Thompson submachine, the classic Tommy gun of the FBI, with the Browning Automatic Rifle, with the A-6 machine gun, with the M-2 carbine. I had a good trigger finger. I could squeeze off one round at a time on a fully automatic weapon. I was also quite accurate from the hip.

The only weapon I didn't do well with was a .45 pistol. Its kick was so violent, and it was so loud, and it bruised my hand so severely, that by the end of a day's target practice with a .45 pistol, I would have to squeeze to avoid losing the gun, and I would send a series of shots off up in the air before I could get control of it enough to make it stop shooting in my hand.

I was well trained. At five hundred yards, I hit a twenty-inch bull's eye ten times out of ten. I could stand with a rifle at my shoulder at a hundred yards and average seven or eight out of ten bull's eyes. But I had no use for all of that training. In Korea, whenever I was in combat situations, I always seemed to lose my gun and carry stretchers. My entire lifetime's accumulation of reading adventure stories and training with weapons were completely lost and useless to me the first time I saw someone shot. I could think of nothing in the world more important than to help that person who was shot; the idea of shooting still more people seemed unthinkable to me, even in the combat heat.

I didn't even get to show my father. When I came home from the Marine Corps and we walked out in the desert behind our house, each of us carrying a gun, firing at targets of opportunity—beercans, bottles, clumps of dirt or grass—my father once again showed that he could stand casually and offhand, and outshoot me, constantly.

I am not paranoid about guns. But from this viewpoint, I want to say that a gun may not cause violence, but guns cause death. To continue to sell an unlimited supply of all the guns you want into a culture that is propagandized many hours a day by television and movies that it is somehow all right or normal to kill, is to create a situation where crime will be, possibly not more prevalent, but much more deadly. Even a fit of rage, one person venting their rage fully on another person, beating them into insensibility, probably won't cause more damage than can be healed in a couple of weeks. But if there is a weapon in the situation, a moment's whim can be accomplished in a second's action. The human being is not easy to kill. It is difficult to kill a human being. But a gun makes it easy. That is wrong. That is a wrongness to loose on society in the name of production and commerce and profit. I don't think it is possible or practical to go collect up all the guns in our society. There are, I am sure, hundreds of thousands of people like my father who, although they have a veritable arsenal stashed away somewhere in their house, are not violent people, and are not made violent by owning guns; but I do know that the country has a love affair with the gun, from the Colt Peacemaker to the .45 to the Derringer to the Saturday Night Special.

When I was in Canada recently, I was asked,

69

"Why do you Americans have all those guns?"

My first answer was,

"I don't have any."

But I was not allowed this easy cop-out. I had to answer for America and their guns, whether I had any or not.

They said, "You have fifty thousand guns down there."

I said, "That's not nearly as many as we have down there."

Sure enough, when I saw the article he had read, it was fifty million guns, not fifty thousand.

I had to explain to the Canadians why the Constitution said we could have guns. They did not understand. It was amusing when I pointed out to them that the reason the Constitution said we could have guns was so the British couldn't come and take us back. It stopped the audience cold. They were stunned and thoughtful as they considered that, those who still live under a monarchy.

Circumstances alter cases; time alters circumstances. We are not going to defend ourselves from the British coming to get us, or the Russians, or anyone else, with a bunch of sporting rifles and pistols. It is not on this level that the battle is joined. It is an illusion to convince the people that they are safer from foreign aggression because they have a bunch of rifles and pistols. Their rifles and pistols and their laughably small sporting supply of ammunition, as compared with a wartime supply of ammunition, are strategically unimportant in a modern war.

Some Americans have reason to fear the Saturday Night Special. But many more Americans have reason to fear the cruise missile, the intercontinental ballistics missile, the MX missile, the multiply-targeted re-entry vehicle missile, the neutron bomb; all are much more potentially deadly than the Winchesters and Remingtons and Colts and Smith & Wessons floating around in our culture. Handguns are a symbol of a sickness; they are a symptom. But they are not the disease. The disease is far more deadly than they are.

I don't think registration and licensing is unreasonable. The National Rifle Association tells us that registration and licensing would make it hard for people to have guns. We register and license automobiles, and everybody has one. When an automobile is used in the commission of a crime, we can sometimes see what its plates are, and its registration has a description, which can aid us to find and track that person down. It would do the same thing with a gun; it is not unreasonable to consider the registration and licensing of handguns.

I know that some people will think I am right-wing or soft on guns because I don't advocate a more punitive or restrictive path. But I don't think a question of this material plane magnitude can be attacked without material plane considerations. Once again, the question arises of who is the criminal: the undereducated, undertrained, laid-off, unemployed holdup man with the .38 in his hand, or the clean, well-bathed, sweet smelling executive somewhere in his drawing room, who made and sold millions of them for business?

We have the multinational corporations selling weapons around the world. Phillip Habib is shuttling between Israel and Lebanon trying to make peace, and we have a large number of salesmen from Lockheed, Rockwell, Boeing, Grumman, trying to sell them the stuff to make war with, while Habib is one guy trying to get them to stop.

Years ago, owning a Thompson submachine gun was a federal offense which would put the FBI on your front doorstep immediately. Now, every paramilitary movement carries automatic weapons that should be illegal at a federal level, and the presence of these weapons is somehow seen as less of a threat than a few inch-and-a-half-barrel thirty-two six-shooters floating around the inner city.

The automatic weapons in the paramilitary groups already have strong laws forbidding their presence in the general public; and if these laws were enforced at the level they should be enforced, many citizens would feel less paranoia in their lives, and possibly less reason to own a handgun.

I don't like to see the right wing arming themselves and organizing paramilitary groups; I also don't like to see the

Jews arming themselves and organizing as a paramilitary group; and I also don't like to see any hippy survivalists arming themselves and organizing as a paramilitary group. I don't want to see any black people buying guns and organizing as a paramilitary group. I don't want anybody to do that. I will defend *anyone's* right to their opinions; but I am not willing to defend anyone's guns.

I am a pacifist and do not support any kind of violence; I think we must move for political, humanitarian, creative solutions rather than military solutions. With the cruel logic of the Mafia and television hostage stories, even if you can't make a brave man quit, you can find somebody that he'll give it up for, some kind of hostage to take. Some kinds of terrorism fall into becoming the people's weapon, the way fire is the people's weapon. When the big guys come on with their Huey helicopters and infrared night-sniper laser-aimed machine guns, the poor people go for what they have—a level of brutality that is possible to throw terror.

Terrorist is a technical term. When Haig talks about El Salvadoran and Guatemalan peasants as being terrorist, he is misusing the term. The real terrorists there are the right-wing death squads who are trying to control the peasants by decimation. That is the classic terrorist tactic, and that is terrorism as a political tactic. The people's attempts are a kind of counter-terrorism. What they can do is to pop a general once in a while, to make it so the ruling heads don't lie easy. I hate to see it. It doesn't make anything feel any better. It makes them use better security and it makes them be worse when they come back on the people again; it escalates it on both sides. That is exactly what Tolstoi meant when he said the difference between revolutionary violence and establishment violence is the difference between dogshit and catshit.

When you come right down to it, the greatest terrorists of all are the ones who come over in helicopters spraying defoliants and fire and chemicals and bombs, and throw terror down, not just on a general or a vice president of a big company, but spread randomly on women, children, and the people. Haig is a terrorist. The Russians in Afghanistan are terrorists. U.S.A. and U.S.S.R. are the top-dog terrorists, under the system we are running right now. Begin is a terrorist and dishonors Israel. And as long as we have someone like Haig—who has no public mandate, as far as I am concerned, to do violence in the name of the American people—America is a country held hostage. We've been held hostage for a long time. The whole world is being held hostage against our behavior.

Pacifism and Foreign Policy

I saw a new piece of equipment on the television: a motorized foxhole in which you can carry a mortar around—a small, armored personnel carrier with a small, open flatbed with a mortar sitting in the middle of it. A motorized mortar. A moving foxhole. This is what we have raised ourselves to. We can make our hole in the ground mobile instead of stationary. How far we have risen.

It is interesting that our foreign policy toward the world is absolutely backwards for the optimum realization of the only viable future which exists for us. The vast majority, ninety percent, of military, economic and legal power in the world is being used to preserve the economic and political boundaries between countries while destroying the cultural and linguistic differences that made the countries rich as cultural well-springs for the world. It is obvious that we need to turn around and begin to preserve the cultural and linguistic differences in the countries while destroying the political, military and economic boundaries between them. It is an obvious case of the old order defining ever more oppression to maintain its ways which are doomed, one way or the other.

In this age of great communication, the people of the world need to communicate one to another, not through their countries, but as human beings to human beings. None of the people in any of the countries want to fight. Some of them may want to be richer, or starve less; or if they think they are going to be attacked, they may want to be more secure; but none of them wants to fight.

The United States reflects the world economy. We were the amplifiers of the industrial revolution: it started in England and came to the United States, where it got automated and fancy and huge. We used to have the biggest everything, the biggest open hearth steel furnace, the biggest forge hammer. And we don't any more. Japan has that. We used to have the most automated assembly lines, and we don't any more. We used to put out the best cars in the world; and we don't any more. And while this is happening, France goes socialist and Poland's officials are afraid the Russian Army is going to come in to straighten the Poles for not holding their workers together better.

If our foreign policy was based on the simple level of our relationship to a country, our country to that country—the United States to Mexico, the United States to Guatemala—and if we treated each one of those countries justly, we could have the freedom for normal diplomatic moves. If we saw a country that was so bloody handed that we couldn't face it, we could drop diplomatic relations with it. We don't have to recognize every government, whether it's cool or not. But every government we could, we should maintain relationships with as long as we possibly can. If we dealt justly with each individual country in that fashion, those countries would become convinced of the advantages of western-style freedom. But the reason those countries are not convinced of the advantages of Western-style freedom is because we have treated those countries expediently, as pawns on an international, planetary level. We have toppled other people's governments and put all kinds of heavy changes on other people's countries, as if the people of those countries had no memory, and as if the people who were ruined in the countries we did that to would not curse the United States for the rest of their lives.

The world has seen us do *stupid* moves, one after the other. One, to get rid of Mossadegh, to not support the Shah when the government was failing, and then to not support the guy who took over after the Shah, and not to support the guy who took over after *him*. That's just casting the country away as an international ally, casting it away.

Reagan is avoiding making the first mistake in El Salvador; he is not going to fail to support the *junta*. Reagan is in the position of trying to prove a philosophy. He has ways he thinks it should work out, and he is looking for a way and a place to use them, to show how they work. An actor looking for a stage to try out his script on.

The question of militarism is contaminated by the actions of the foreign policy sultans of our government, who have been making their foreign policy decisions on the basis of organizing the world to fight Russia, instead of taking care of and preserving the liberties of the countries which were in our economic and political aura. We have defended Somoza. He was one of ours; he went to West Point. We have defended Somoza in Nicaragua, and the Shah in Iran. We have defended one dictator after another around the world, and they have to do something really gross before we drop them. When Bokassa used all his foreign aid in one chunk to blow out on his coronation, then we decided, well, if he's going to set himself up as a complete Napoleon-living-God-king, taking the entire gross national product to give himself a coronation, we'll cut his foreign aid off. But other than that, they'll go ahead and support the grossest kind of thing, as long as it doesn't be communist. This is one of the causes of unrest and revolution through all the world.

If the big First World countries would stop manufacturing arms and shipping them to Third World countries, the Third World countries wouldn't have such bad wars. Before Russia got into Afghanistan, the Afghanis used to file their rifles out from stock, file them out by eyeball. But now there's a nice, brisk trade in automatic weapons.

You get countries who make and sell weapons for no other reason than for the pure money of it, interfering in other people's business.

In Nicaragua, to get what they got, they lost almost a generation of teenagers. Somoza's army would come up and just machine gun bus stops full of teenagers on the grounds that the teenagers were probably going to be with the Sandinistas. They really lost a lot doing that.

We know that the line the government is putting out is bull. We know that the cause of the problems in Guatemala, El Salvador, and all those countries is not Cuba, is not communism, is not Russia; is the oppression of the native people by the local military governments. I have been to Guatemala eight times since 1976, and lived six weeks in the goat lane behind a village. The guerrillas are the local folks; and the reason it is hard to stop them is that in the territory they own, they are completely supported by the people. They are not outside anything. They are the local folks, and the local people feed them and shelter them and take care of them.

Some of the worst ills committed against the innocent and helpless undeveloped and third world countries of the world have been at the borders. The borders are where your very being-ness is wrong. When you come as a refugee from El Salvador to Texas, you are treated as an undesirable criminal. Our country says it takes political refugees. They say they don't take economic refugees because, obviously, the world is so poor that we would be inundated. So we will limit ourselves to political refugees: those people who are being oppressed. Yet, in the first few months of 1981, twelve hundred Salvadorans are in jail in all the county jails along the Texas border. Obvious victims of oppression—ours or someone else's—in jail.

A farmer down by the Mexican border says,

"We don't own slaves any more. We just rent them."

We took anybody Castro sent us because he was Communist. And he became so cynical that he emptied his jails and mental institutions on us. But legitimate refugees fleeing for their lives overland across the tropical and desert length of Mexico as far as the United States is across, to the great golden door, are ushered into jail and sent back to face the death squads.

The borders of the United States don't keep Arab oilmen

from buying American farmland. Money crosses the border with no problems at all. Ownership of the land can cross the border without any problem at all.

Some of the secret is that the world pirates contain the sovereignty of nations, not the people.

South Africa declared Bophuthatswana a sovereign country. What that really means is that they can starve to death, and South Africa is not responsible to feed them, because they are living in a sovereign country. They have free will. But the only jobs are outside Bophuthatswana and the border was not placed by the workers; had they a choice, their work and their homes would remain in the same country. They have, as a people, no sovereignty. Their nation is a caricature of public sovereignty.

It is a grand thing that one can travel from one side of this country to the other without anything more serious than an agricultural inspection. It is one of the ways in which what we are doing in this country works right. But it is very interesting to note that of the countries of the world, America is one of the worst borders to cross, and that in general the countries of the Empire—the Anglo-American British Empire—are some of the most difficult borders in the world, especially the darker your skin.

In Europe, the passing from country to country is frequently no more difficult than the agricultural check between Arizona and New Mexico. They realize that people must travel. It is shown by the way in which Americans and Europeans carry their passports. The American carries the passport sealed away in the deepest pocket of the deepest, darkest compartment of his bag; a European frequently carries his passport on a chain around his neck, where it can be read quickly by the guard as he walks freely through the border station with his luggage in his hands, on to do his legitimate business, and not hindered much at the border. It is good that we can move freely from state to state in America; but America could learn from Europe about how to move from country to country.

When we ask the pacifist/militarist question, on the

pacifist side we get to say that we can do some smart international moves, instead of a Neanderthal foreign policy that leaves us in such a condition with everybody mad at us that we have to, as a country, sleep with a gun under our pillow because we have angered the world.

The assumption between the right wingers and the American government is that the right wingers in the Russian government are always going to prevail. If there wasn't a lot of oppression going on, there wouldn't be a lot of revolution going on. Folks don't run a revolution in countries that aren't pretty oppressed. It's not worthwhile. You can't get anybody mad enough.

Guatemala was going to have a revolution two or three years ago. But everybody said, "No, Guatemala's not going to go off right now, because business is actually pretty good; and if you can't get the businessmen mad enough, you can't bring a revolution off." In Nicaragua, there were a lot of businessmen who didn't like it that Somoza had Coca Cola and Jeep and Land Rover and all the franchises that were valuable in the country. They didn't like it at all.

Instead of Somoza and his family, it's maybe a hundred families. But the net effect to the people is the same as if it were just one guy running it, in Guatemala and El Salvador.

What we didn't do about Korea the first time, which could have saved us having the entire Korean War, we are now not doing about Korea again. We are once again stepping in and supporting a dictator. They say the good thing about this dictator is that he allowed himself to be entreated to give his predecessor life in prison rather than the death penalty.

He gets to go shake hands with our President. But our President also did Van Heusen shirt ads. He'll do anything.

The prevailing attitude in the United States is that third world countries let the PLO address the UN because they're all a bunch of wogs anyway, and the wogs help each other out. This is your basic Republican viewpoint on why the PLO got to address the UN.

What they don't understand is that a hundred thirty small nations are not all run by corrupt people who would blow

80

with the wind and who don't do anything except knee-jerk support each other. There are people of great integrity who have come out of the third world. Secretary-General U Thant, for example, came from a third world country. People like that have become famous in the world forum. The third world countries are morally as big as the United States and Russia. It is a hypocrisy on the part of the United States and Russia to pretend otherwise.

The industrial revolution has put the screws on the world to the point where the whole world protests and squeaks and groans. It is a wrong path, and it is one that needs to be climbed down from.

You think it's hard to get one person to climb down and admit they were wrong. It's really hard to get a culture to climb down. You can find a thousand experts who say you shouldn't.

The funny thing about the Republicans who want the USA out of the UN is that the only people who want out of the UN worse than the Republicans are the Communists, who can't stand the UN any better than the Republicans. Russia can't stand the UN any better than the United States can, because they turn around and jump off on Russia over Afghanistan just as fast as they jump off on the United States about El Salvador. There is some justice in what those small countries are saying. I hope no one was offended by my earlier reference to wogs, but I was trying to illustrate the racist nature of the agreement.

If the worst-case scenario writers have their way, the Great Depression and the results of the wars over the diminishing supply will reduce human culture fifty or seventy-five years back into its development. If the country doesn't change its ways, the ways are going to change naturally through a great economic collapse across the whole world. We are suspended on a very high level of technology; it doesn't take very much hassle to mess that technology and set us back about forty years. All that delicate hardware that the system is suspended on requires a very high level of integration. As it becomes fancier and more technological, it becomes less

81

and less able to support that level. In the best case, the enlightened world-sharing and distribution of the resources on an equitable basis will so enhance the standard of living of all the countries of the world that the necessity for militarily guarded political boundaries will wither away in the true communication/computer-caused withering away of the state.

These are the basic alternatives. The others are limited land warfare for the next hundred years, immediate spasm atomic destruction of the entire civilized world, with the resultant fallout damage to the remainder of the third world which did not participate in the immediate war; or the destruction and waste of farmland and fuel supplies to the point of causing Lebensraum wars all over the planet.

Don't think we can't have a hundred-years war. The only thing that would keep us from having a hundred-years war would be if we destroyed ourselves first. We've had hundred-years wars before. We've had thirty-years wars. This is the direction in which they are pointing us.

Not A Company Man

My father used to work for a large construction company in San Bernardino where, because he was a very experienced craftsman, builder, carpenter, journeyman in several aspects of the construction craft, he rose quickly to become foreman of the shop. It was a large construction company, and the shop was where they did the cabinetry for homes that were built. Occasionally, the company might build a penitentiary or a library with all the cabinetry. they once built a courtroom.

There was a job at hand which was on the owner's personal house. The owner had a few pieces of special wood that he wanted for his house, and one of the men who worked for my father in the cabinet shop made a mistake in calculation and sawed a piece of expensive wood in a way so as to waste some of it.

Later on, the owner came in and found that this particular piece of wood, which he had taken quite a fancy to, had been damaged. He got angry and started raising hell, and wanted my father to fire the man who had done that.

My father said,

"You know, I'm real good at running this shop here. I've saved you thousands of dollars by being more than ordinarily careful with the materials here. I've saved you such a lot of money that I don't think it would be appropriate to fire one of these men for a not-really-terribly-expensive piece of wood."

The owner of the company said,

"Floyd, you're real good at what you do, and you're pretty far up into the company now. I think it's time that you made a choice, whether you're a company man or not."

Floyd said that he didn't feel like he could fire one of those men; those men had families, and it was too lightweight a thing to fire them over, to make them lose their job over an expensive piece of wood.

The owner told him to make his choice, whether he was a company man or not.

My father said he guessed he wasn't, and was fired on the spot. The next day, another man at the company, a friend of my father's who had been promoted to fill his job, called up my father and said,

"I know you're buying a house out there and you can't afford to let the payments lapse, and you can't afford to be out of work. I'll offer you a job, because if you can't come back and work as a carpenter for me, they'll have to fire me, too."

My father thought it over and made that kind of choice that people have to make who live in civilization, and went back to work for that company as a common carpenter, in order to keep a weekly check happening, in order to keep making the payments.

I've always respected those moves.

Business is Business

Having economics be a primary determiner of public policy is a perversion of the Constitution. Business is the real church of this country. The real philosophy is, business is business. The laws are bent to help business. The ethic of that goes back to the idea of earning a living: that a man should not be denied the opportunity to earn a living—free enterprise. But the question of free enterprise is the same as the question of why wine is 12.5 per cent alcohol. The yeast and bacteria are given free enterprise to expand until they produce a solution of 12.5 per cent alcohol, which kills them all.

Business is business. We will sell guns for business. We will make dioxin for business. American chemical companies make more pesticides than those that are legal to be used in the United States, knowingly, every year, and export them. They make about twice as many amphetamines as are legally sold each year. They know that the overflow is being sold over the counter in countries like Mexico and the third world, and going out as dope. The Pinto case and the faulty gearshift levers point up the philosophy that Ford Motor Company was following: it was cheaper to pay the damages for the people killed by their cars than it was to modify the cars and make them safe. That is a typical economic attitude, firmly based in the maximizing of profit.

The villain in all this, although rarely recognized or called by its right name, is greed. Greed was legislated against in the Bible. They called it usury, the charging of high interest rates. In the U.S., many states had anti-usury laws, and the state legislatures quietly struck down the anti-usury laws so the interest rates could soar beyond what was defined as usury. In the old days, usury was considered a crime. We have now reached levels of usury that would have been considered criminal and actionable fifteen or twenty years ago. Once again, when it comes to push and shove, even the Bible rolls over, and business is what is really sacrosanct.

The prime interest rate is purely in the hands of the government economists, which is not free market. You can be kept from access to the financial capital; you can just be blocked from access to capital. Whole classes of people can. Of course, the real rich don't care. They don't need to borrow money. The people who are hurt are the people who have to borrow money to buy a television set.

Gross national product is a wrong indicator of the prosperity and wealth of the country. A lot of the things that make for prosperity at the lower income levels do not even show in the Gross National Product, such as people who grow gardens, or people who fix cars for themselves, or people who build their own housing, or people who recycle things at an individual level, or people who live economically. Yet those are the things that make a difference in people's lifestyles. Some people are now starting clubs of bartering. They reduce their Gross Family Product drastically in terms of money, and in terms of the things measured by the Gross National Product; but they may be living more prosperously than someone with a higher Gross Family Product, because they are into bartering, and they trade goods for services and services for goods, making all sorts of arrangements through which no money flows and in which there are no taxes to be paid, arrangements which truly help out the health and well-being of the family, without adding to the formal Gross Family Product. These are the kinds of projects that need to be taken care of in the United States, rather than building cars or building tanks or building airplanes, or building bridges, because those things raise the Gross National

Product while contributing more entropy, not adding to the well-being of the people.

The free market system directly implies that, although we are not collective, the enlightened self-interest of a business-man would cause him to put his money out to work and to return it to the community, that a stronger community might result, capable of generating more money and making more profit. What are we to say when the people who have the access to and control of the money control it in such a way as to allow the inner circles of our big cities to die, because the people who live in them are dark? What sort of stewardship is that?

John D. Rockefeller said that he felt he was commanded by God to make as much money as he possibly could, and to use it to help straighten out the world. He felt that was a commandment from God.

In the *Saturday Evening Post* when I was growing up, there was a series of stories, Earthworm tractors vs. Behemoth tractors. Earthworms were Caterpillars. The guy from Behemoth was unprincipled, and would do anything. Kind of like Tugboat Annie stories: a hot independent could go out and compete with the big outfit. Tugboat Annie was always in competition with a guy from another tugboat outfit, who was a lot bigger and richer than she was, and had a lot more boats.

The fiction of the country was for the underdog. These are the kind of stories that were between the covers that Rockwell drew.

That was the vision of free enterprise that we had during World War II, and immediately afterwards. There was a place in it, even up to *Giant*, the Edna Ferber book about the wildcatter, Jet Rink, getting so rich that the old established cattle folks had to recognize him socially though they hated it.

The myth of the free market assumes some parity among the horsetraders. In olden times, there were proscriptions against usury that were in effect from the church, when usury was against the law. Not only usury, but there was a

level short of usury which was considered, if not a legal
matter, at least an ecclesiastical matter, and people would be
warned against the un-Christian nature of "sharp practices."
Sharp practices included the kind of farming mentality that
confused husbandry with being sure to plant the fruit trees
on the side of the property close to the fence, so the shade
would fall on your neighbor's property and the fruit would
fall on your own. At that level, there are many things that
could be done by a farmer that could be considered "sharp
practices." But the Bible taught that the first two rows along
the edge of the road were dedicated to passing travelers who
in those days of non-frozen or concentrated foods, could not
possibly carry enough food for a very long journey, and
probably didn't have any actual money on their persons as
they traveled. These were cultural norms. Some may say that
is naive and it was easier then, and there are more people
now and times are harder. But two rows alongside the field
of a giant complicated farm is virtually insignificant. There
are huge quantities of food produced and harvested these
days, but two rows could still be done without damage to the
industry. It is merely that sharp practices have become
"normal", which is to say not right or acceptable, but done
by so many people that the curve describing the frequency of
that action is near the norm.

Another of the messages which come from the business-
man's political party is the sort of message that was sent by
Richard Milhous Nixon when he became a millionaire while
in office. After all, all his friends were millionaires; he was
the only one of the bunch who wasn't a millionaire. The least
he could do was to become a millionaire while in office. It's
part of the act.

It's like the scandal around Lyn Nofziger, one of the
President's oldest advisers, who was recently exposed as a
slumlord around Washington and Maryland. He bought
property up on the advice of Washington speculators, who
had been advising the inside circle that it was a good
investment. Those on the inside had been buying up that
kind of land. It was the Administration's way of paying off

the loyal soldiers, to let out information on which a profit could be made. To a businessman, everything is negotiable. It would have been considered a great shame to have friends in high positions, and know the right people, and not get the information to make a profit.

Nofziger pleaded ignorance: he was only following the orders of his investment counselors. Imagine the scene:

Bucky Fuller points out that the pirates on the ocean were above governments and established the market. Ambrose Bierce said, "Piracy is commerce, just as God made it, without all the fol-de-rols." The capitalistic philosophers were basically the materialist philosophers who had not found God in the Universe—not recognizing that God *is* the Universe—and declared God a *latifundista*, or absentee landlord. Practicality was enshrined above morality. Pragmatism became not realism but piracy.

The myth is that the free market will right itself. Supply and demand are a law, so they say. Yet we see plainly that although there is a planetary glut of petroleum and the market is stagnant, that the price of gasoline continues to climb. This shows that the "law" of supply and demand has been repealed by the interaction of government and the oil business.

Ayn Rand talks about the difference between making money and creating wealth, making something more valuable. That was the idea of the materialistic philosophers: that man's hand on the environment made it more valuable. But that assumed that there was an unlimited supply of land, trees, rocks, whatnot. We are now faced with the reality that entropy exists in the business world, too.

During the last Depression, the money guys figured out how to loot the ship. So the government set up laws to keep the money guys from being able to loot the ship. Now the money guys have all different ways figured out about how to loot the ship, and there aren't any laws about the ways they have figured out to loot the ship now. It will take years and years of litigation before anyone can decide whether or not the ways they are now looting the ship are legal. And by the time they get done with that, they'll probably have the ship looted so badly that it won't float again, and we'll have a Depression. This has become the legal profession's primary occupation: to figure out how the big money may continue to loot the ship, against the intentions and will of the crew.

Reagan says he defends freedom; but he doesn't defend anything free. He just defends their right to loot the ship. And there isn't a strong advocacy on the other side, saying, "Don't let them loot our ship!"

Roosevelt applied WPA like a tourniquet to stop us from bleeding to death. The guys who have come since Roosevelt have applied so many tourniquets in so many directions that they tend to stop circulation. They are not doing it from a motive of saving the country like Roosevelt; they are doing it from knowing that it has worked in the past and will probably work again. But the truth about that kind of magic spell is that every time it is used, it is less effective, until you reach a point at which it has no effect at all.

In a way, it is almost a moot point whether the pirates are looting the ship worse than the liberals are. This is the traditional Republican viewpoint. The liberals are letting the money out onto projects which are to help out; but once you have a machinery by which projects may be initiated, then people will develop the skill of getting money via those grants and procedures, until people can take each grant criterion and push it out to its farthest limit. By pushing all the criteria for grants around, you can rig it so money gets given away for some of the silliest things imaginable, which Senator Proxmire is continually freaking out about in the *National Enquirer*. They are giving away gigantic grants, millions of dollars, for projects that seem designed to keep a bunch of Ph.D.'s and laboratory technicians employed. It's a form of welfare.

I used to feel that my job was to run along the bottom of the bloated government with an icepick, poking holes in it so it would leak out. I thought that was what a liberal was supposed to do: bring the government down faster. But the government's so huge that those little leaks are never going to kill it; they're just going to make it a little sick and inefficient.

We have to look for the real welfare cheaters, like the people who develop multimillion dollar weapons systems that get scrapped after the prototype is built. Talk about wasteful. Having Lockheed and Boeing and Rockwell all build their own version of the Cruise missile is absurd in the first place; and the amount of backbiting and industrial spying that goes on among the companies themselves is almost as bad as the amount of backbiting and spying that goes on among the countries. And the price of it gets added into the contracts.

Business is business. A cost overrun is more business. The right wingers say they are against welfare, but the cost overruns on nuclear power plants are no different than welfare to the construction companies, the architects: white collar welfare for the Ph.D.'s. The $40 billion subsidy to the nuclear industry is a gross form of welfare.

The businesses are in intensive care! The Benzene decision, for example, is a case of propping up a market for a company which otherwise would fail. The real nature of the free market is that a lot of businesses fail; the ones that are dishonest or harmful go under. But the present system subsidizes the dishonest and harmful industries, by relaxing the regulations controlling emissions and poisons into the environment.

These subsidies are costs which represent the hidden failures of the free market system.

Agriculture is another field in which the sanctity of business takes precedence over all other things. Not only does the government tell you what to plant; but the criteria it uses to tell you what to plant are economic, rather than human ones. For example, pension funds for the American Medical Association are invested in a very large portfolio, which includes about three per cent tobacco companies. The AMA invests in tobacco because it makes money for their pension funds. The tobacco industry is supported by this; the government even pays subsidies to tobacco farmers, for business reasons. We could tell the farmers, "Instead of planting tobacco, plant your acreage in food to feed the poor, and we'll subsidize you at the same rate as tobacco." It would give the same amount of money to the farmer, feed the poor, not contribute to spreading cancer throughout the population, and improve the land.

The corporation idea of organization has forgotten that one of the basic reasons for all of these endeavors is for us to come together and have something to do that is a way to earn a living, to save us from crying in the streets for our bread. An efficiency that reduces the work force as well as the quality of the goods harms the body of the creature.

It is obvious that the tampering with industry by government and advertising and the corporations to fulfill their needs removes the economy from the sphere of what is called free market. We should admit that our economy is a controlled economy. Since it is a controlled economy, how about if we remove some of the corruption from it, if it is ours to control. Under the current system, the benefits to the public of the free market system are subverted by the maximization of profit. According to the free market system, if someone can come along with a better product at a lower price, they should be able to take over the market Then, if the industry happens to create a better product to get the market back, this is healthy competition, and is good for the free enterprise system. This, however, is not what happens when a new product is introduced.

If product "A" can be sold on the market at ninety-eight cents, and a new product is initiated, it will probably sell on the market at ninety-five cents, even though it was manufactured at fifteen cents, because the pricing will not be predicated on the true cost of production, but on the projected price of the competition, including a fat advertising budget and many high-salaried executives. Maximization of profits dictates that new products not depress the market. This is how, when God makes it dry the farmers have a bad year. When God makes it rain, it makes it a good year. Then man takes a good year and depresses the market and turns it into a bad year. If the people have a bad year when God makes a drought and the people have a bad year when God gives them rain, when do the people have a good year?

We are really on the horns of a dilemma. On one side, government doesn't run very well. Graft, corruption, loss of money, boondoggle, waste, etc. I am not talking about taking over the government. I am not talking about a state collectivity. We have a state collectivity now which is the commonwealth of the United States, which we citizens own collectively, and which the politicians presume to burn some of once in a while to hot up the economy. I don't care for the state any better because it says it is a collective state instead of a capitalist state. I just don't trust the state very well.

And on the other horn, the multinational corporations are so awesome in their power that only the state is within striking distance of any regulation of business whatsoever. Business runs, supposedly, on enlightened self-interest. I think in the last fifteen years or so we have seen that enlightenment still retains its mystique, by reason of its rarity despite the huge burst of religious thought in the sixties. Enlightened altruism is extremely difficult to find. Enlightened self-interest is rarer yet.

The money-making ethic, which I assume we must call capitalism, has spread to where it affects the killing of the seals on the edge of Newfoundland for furs to make coats. Fifteen or twenty years ago, they used to kill fifty thousand seals a year. Now they can't find that many, and the yearly kill has fallen to twenty thousand because they have thinned them out so badly. Not only are the Newfoundlanders killing them, but the Norwegians are coming all the way from Norway to kill them. Moreover, the American and Canadian and Russian fishing industries are fishing out the fish in the area so badly that they are competing with the seals for something to eat. The seals are in an awful position; they are not getting enough to eat on one end, and on the other end the Norwegians and Canadians are killing them wholesale when they attempt to breed and reproduce.

The seals live in an extremely hostile ecology. They are a

miraculous piece of life force, evolved to live without hands or feet in an environment as inhospitable as the north seas, perfectly defenseless, except for their ability to swim away fast. And they are so preyed upon for the purpose of making money that, although perfectly fitted to survive in that environment, they are no longer able to do so.

The inability of the white seals to survive in their ecology is identical with the inability of the Guatemalan Indians to survive where they have been for thousands and thousands of years. The system which they evolved to live there was destroyed by a money-making system which was substituted for it, and which does not work as well.

When you read the histories of the discovery and conquest of Mexico and Peru, Hernando Cortez and Pizarro, it doesn't really make it plain what a high level of civilization was destroyed by the *conquistadores*. Some of the cities of the Maya which were destroyed were older and bigger than the cities in Europe where those *conquistadores* had come from. Their calendar was more accurate.

The web of citizenry and ecology in Peru, for instance, was so highly evolved that, in that mountainous land, there was a level of crops and a kind of corn evolved for every altitude change from the coast to the fifteen- and twenty-thousand-foot peaks by Machu Picchu. There was a kind of corn that grew at every altitude, and there was commerce all the way from those peaks down to the ocean.

The way the society was designed was beautiful, elegant in its efficiency. There were people who always lived at the beach. There were people who always lived in the foothills. There were people who always lived in the low mountains; and there were people who always lived in the high mountains. The people who lived in an area would carry goods across their own territory, to which they had become adapted over ages of time. When it got to the edge of the foothills, the beach people would set it down, and the low-altitude ones would pick it up and carry it up to the middle altitudes, across their own territory. They would then set it down and it would go across the next territory by people who lived in the middle altitudes all the time, and were adapted to it.

It took thousands of years to develop a system with a kind of corn for every level of altitude, and a kind of people for every level of altitude. When the Spanish came in and conquered that country, it was not a military feat, but merely the destruction of that beautiful system, which worked better than the one that is there now.

These are gross examples of the breakdown of systems all over the world. Western civilization is an entropy maker, a trash producer, an inflation generator, a war-profiteer and a misery maker. People who defend it are ignorant, because they do not understand what it has done to the world.

It is kinder to starve because the weather was bad than to starve because somebody made a mistake, or somebody was greedy and took your livelihood away. Grief is easier to bear when it comes from God than when it comes from man. Man is very arrogant to make his grief and his affliction be heavier on mankind than the affliction that God had already allotted for mankind.

California Turnaround

We were coming back from California, taking the northern route in our old Scenicruiser, running fast at eight thousand feet. The bus was tuned for lower altitudes, and was putting out a little black smoke. Early in the morning around sunrise, with no one awake but Wilbur, the driver, and me sitting shotgun, a trucker pulled up behind us.

"Who's that great big white bus putting out that long trail of black smoke?" came over our radio.

We talked back to him, and he talked to us on the radio as he overtook us. He was obviously loaded on some truckdriver speed. Maybe black beauties, or what they call "California turnaround," meaning you can drive to California and turn around and drive back.

His speed was so strong as he pulled up behind our bus, he said so much fast jive talk, and so many quick and funny things and so much noise and so much speed and blew by us so fast that he woke up everybody on our bus. People came up to the front and watched his truck disappear off into the distance, as awake as if they had all had a cup of coffee.

That was a fast trucker. He had so much speed he woke up everybody as he passed and left them sitting in his wake rubbing their eyes and wondering how come they were so awake. Speed is catching. By the time that trucker had taken his lonely ball of speed past our bus, he had contacted twenty-five or thirty people into instant wakefulness.

Automobiles & Addiction

To understand the love affair of the American with the automobile is to realize that it is an addiction. Aldous Huxley said there has only been one new sin invented since the original seven deadly sins; that new sin is *speed*.

Speed in this usage is quite an interesting term. Amphetamine addicts, methedrine addicts referred to their crystalline chemical partner as *speed*, and people who understood the nature of speed used to make buttons that said, *Speed kills*. Folks who were into methedrine understood that it didn't just mean cars, and that it did kill.

Part of the lure of mechanical speed relates to the fact of our binocular vision—our brain contains a depth-perceiving computer—and we are descended, God help me for mentioning it, from brachiate animals, that is, creatures that can swing through the trees. I don't say this merely to anger the special creationists, but on the circumstantial evidence of binocular vision and the opposable thumb.

I think it just feels good for our kind of creature to try out our depth-perceiving computer by running it fast down a row of trees or a row of fence posts or a row of telephone poles or a row of other cars; the more interesting the scenery is that we drive through, the more pressure of accomplishment is pressed against that small, accurate computer there in the back of our mind. It likes to be stimulated. All our computers like to be stimulated. There's always something meditational for me to drive down the road and project myself for about a quarter-mile out the windshield down the road ahead of me, taking it all in. As Lawrence of Arabia said of a motorcycle, what you lose in detail at seventy, you gain in comprehension.

It's not just the accident that a car can be made to go fast; it's that we *like it* to go fast. It's not easy to back us down; it's not easy to slow us down. It's hard to make us quit doing something that feels good. The effect of the automobile on the human psyche is almost exactly the same effect as that of a drug.

Early cars were short, boxy and puny. For the next thirty or forty years, the industry fled to escape this image with longer, lower, wider, more powerful, until it was clear that the cars that were being built were too fast for the existing road system. In a burst of power that may someday be recognized as being comparable to the pyramids or the Great Wall of China, we built an interstate freeway system that covered the entire United States, allowing legal speeds of seventy to seventy-five miles an hour from coast to coast; and in truth, most of the freeway was good for a hundred to a hundred and fifty.

The early, long, low, wide, more powerful cars were underbraked and naively suspended for the speeds and powers invested in them. The first time foreign cars came to the United States, they offered not gas mileage, for gas was cheap; they offered handling, accuracy of steering, sophistication of suspension, responsive engines, transmissions and engines mated to produce useful power curves. For many years, Corvette was held up to ridicule beside the likes of the MG/TC, the TR-3, and the Morgan, any of which, on certain types of winding courses, were the match of the huge V-8.

It was obvious what the disease was as it progressed. After the original 1957 Thunderbird, competitions were held to produce the Thunderbird of the future. The car which was picked as the most innovative design for the Thunderbird of the future was a 1500 c.c. V-4 two-seater which was hailed by the fans of English and Italian sports cars as a breakthrough in the American auto industry, and promptly scrapped in favor of the version of the Thunderbird which grew into a personal limousine with four hundred cubic inches of V-8 under the hood. America was not ready for a 1500 c.c. V-4 Thunderbird of the future.

At the same time as the auto industries were sponsoring drag strips to keep the dragsters off the streets and develop better car technology and improve the design, to sustain all of this high-horsepower automobile racing, they were speaking piously of reducing engine size and ending the horsepower race to save materials, lives and fuel. There was an industry-wide agreement to give up racing.

The Mustang was issued as a prototype of a medium-small gutsy car. The Chevy II was another. Although they were touted as four-cylinder gas savers, the V-8 version took the sales. The car industry began surreptitiously going back on its agreement to end the horsepower race until Ford Motor Company blatantly shattered the intent and spirit of the agreement by fielding a line of computer-designed high-tech Ford V-8 racing engines that ended Offenhauser's domination of the Indianapolis Speedway in a matter of three or four years: outright racing.

The fire caught and flared across the whole United States. 150 mile per hour Dodges. Magnums 440 cubic inches. Five hundred cubic inch Cadillacs. Options that made showroom cars, if not competitive with the supersportsman stockers of the stock car circuit, at least completely sufficient to kill an inexperienced driver on the street. Now Chrysler Corporation wants the government to give them money to make up for the thirty years they spent building space monsters instead of righteously developing transportation that recognized the realities of the world.

We spent fifteen to twenty years in a design slump, ignoring the obvious message of the future, because the resources of the automobile industry were dictated by the sales departments, rather than by the engineering departments. This is the failing of capitalism. This is the level of waste that humankind cannot afford. This is the wrong teaching that the United States spreads upon the whole world. This is the reality that the Republican administration is either unwilling or unable to understand.

During those years when the automobile industry was milking the market for the final few bucks before doing what they knew needed to be done, they continued to keep the ancient monsters hot with the sauce of salesmanship. I remember the first time I saw one car showroom publish a poster of the competition, pointing out its faults. I was so naive that I used to think advertising meant showing why your product was good instead of trying to show how the other product was bad.

The advertisers are using psychology to appeal to drives in us that are damaging to us and damaging to society, for the sake of selling a product to keep the economy at a high level.

We have used sex to sell poison for your Johnson grass and wrenches to fix your tractor; but we use the love of speed to sell automobiles; it is just as immoral as if there were a large government-sponsored respectable organization which sold heroin.

The maximization of profits is what dictates salesmanship, which rigs the system. If the free market is not allowed to run at a normal, healthy and free homeostasis, the maximization of profit has the same effect on the system as a raging fever in an individual who is ill. Circulation increases. Warmth increases. But the extra heat is at the cost of burning the body, in the case of the individual, and the environment in our very real case.

The use of psychology to sell something is basically immoral, and perverts the free market. The supply and demand theory implies a relationship of demand to need. To use psychology in advertising causes people to think there is a need where none really exists, creating an artificial need. It is taught that we need a variety of chemicals, paints, potions, perfumes, pads and pills in order to be a complete person.

The positive side of the capitalist motto was enunciated by Henry J. Kaiser: "Find a need and fill it." But it was assumed that the advertising would be truthful, and that the need would be real, or the consumer would be unable accurately to fulfill his needs.

The pleasurable effect of speed is a function of binocular vision, as well as the kinesthetic senses. Because we have good depth perception, we can drive cars and fly airplanes.

The effect of the feel on the psyche, to be understood, requires an understanding of the difference between heroin and opium, and cocaine/coca leaves, and beer, wine/brandy/ hard liquor.

Andrew Weil points out that many cultures have had stable relationships with plants which remained stable because the relationship was with a plant. The dosage was not artificially increased. As soon as the dosage became artificially increased, the damage to the human being became so strong that the cumulative damage began to affect society, and society began to move against the substances for their *antisocial* effects.

Opium, although less effective than heroin in the reduction of pain, is also less dangerous than heroin in rapidity of addiction. This is because heroin takes the active ingredient of the opium and refines it to chemical purity, and the body is then called upon to deal with a much more powerful mixture of that substance than could be found in nature.

In the same way, Indians in South America have chewed coca leaves for generations; but modern science distills cocaine from the coca leaves, and creates once again a substance much more effective on the nervous system than that found in nature.

Also to be considered are hard liquor and brandy as opposed to the natural fermented drinks, beer and wine: in the Middle Ages, monks in monasteries wrote learned treatises on brandy and how it released the magical effects of the mind, and how it gave wings to their meditation. You would have thought they were talking about eating peyote, or taking LSD.

The thing that is common to the change that took place in opium, cocaine and alcohol was that the concentration of the active ingredient allowed the stimulus that was given to the body to be much more powerful. This is part of the mechanism of addiction. The mind is a very powerful integrative force; it is designed to be able to integrate a variety of situations and conditions and still maintain homeostasis. In order to be "high", there is a disturbance in the homeostasis. The body will try to return to homeostasis, and will soon learn to function in a nearly normal fashion while loaded up with opiates, speed, caffeine, alcohol or a psychedelic. The body will tend by this mechanism to require a stronger stimulus to achieve the same effect.

In that same sense, the amount of speed normal for a naturally evolved human animal would be limited to running, leaping, swinging on swings, high diving—the absolute in kinesthetic stimulation.

The question of stimulation is central. The original seven deadly sins, greed, anger, lust, etc., can be easily seen to imply the gratification of one or another particular sense, even to the damage of the rest of the sensorium. It is possible to see that he who risks mangling his semi-colloid body against the side of a mountain or a tree or an oncoming bridge for the sake of the visual and kinesthetic stimuli available from speed commits a technical sin.

Sometimes I'm not sure whether sin is a subcategory of addiction, or addiction is a subcategory of sin.

When you see how fast most of us move, and what percentage of our ability to integrate gravity, velocity and acceleration we normally use (those of us who are not Nadia Comaneci), it becomes obvious that we are able to integrate a great deal more speed than we would normally run into in the world if it were not for the wheel. The wheel is speed for mankind; speed for the mind; speed for the body. It moves goods faster; it moves communications faster. It is one of the affirming principles on which modern civilization is built, in the most McLuhanesque sense.

Other things are addictive in addition to those substances most people consider addictive drugs. Lenses can be addictive, or junk. Amplification can be addictive. Folks who get hooked in the addictive sense behave in certain ways: there is an addictive kind of behavior. Being a holdup man is an addiction. If you like that kind of juice, if you like seeing people's eyes get wide when they get scared, if you like having a lot of power, if you like to go in and say a couple of magic words, it's an addiction. Like my friend in the next cell said,

"Don't pull back the hammer until you get their attention."

The damaging thing about material/chemical/mechanical speed is that although the organism enjoys it, there are side effects to the body. The long-run result will be a loss rather than a gain. We could have a relationship with the computer and the television much more rewarding than our relationship with the automobile, much less damaging to us in the long run, and much more educational than the repetitive feeling of being thrown against a shoulder harness again and again. If humankind wants to enjoy speed, they have to make the same jump that you make when you go from ordinary reading to speed reading: they have to quit moving their mouths and pointing their fingers and smashing themselves in sports cars, and allow the part of their mind that can *really* speed some freedom.

The Constitution

"It is plain that the Constitution was designed to keep the
government off the backs of the people."
—Justice William O. Douglas
United States Supreme Court

The Constitution was designed as a protection against
tyranny. By a curious paradox, the system that has evolved
from the Constitution now perpetuates the very tyranny the
founding fathers sought to protect against. The Constitution
extends its protection to the citizen against the government
and other intrusions such as the press and corporations,
under color of law or not. The Supreme Court was a product
of the Congress. It is sworn to uphold the Constitution.
Instead, by revering precedent above all else, they have
upheld the "integrity" of the Supreme Court, at the expense
of the common sense which formed the very basis of the
Constitution.

I remember when I was very young I unquestioningly
assumed the attitudes of the country, and when I was told
things that denied that, I refused to believe it or said it was
lies. It was with tremendous shock that I learned of troops
firing on miners in Colorado, and how many times we have
come on violent to union people, how many times we have
sent soldiers out to mow down the unions. I always hated
hearing that stuff, and I didn't believe it. I didn't believe my
country would do that. I was that naive a kid coming out of

school that I *didn't believe any of that stuff had happened.*

After joining the Marine Corps, when I got to Korea, I realized that I had no business there, and that we were messing with these people's country by having a war on top of them, and that a couple of big countries were oppressing a little country by fighting on their territory, and the little country wasn't getting anything out of it, except getting knocked around a bunch and all their buildings torn down and a lot of their people killed. A lot of their fields had to go fallow and fill up with weeds for a few years because they couldn't go into combat zones.

I started hearing stuff from Viet Nam, and I remembered back to the ideas that were implanted in me during World War II. I remembered how the Japanese, "filthy demons" that they were, raped nurses in the Philippines. That was one of the things that I realize now that was run across the country real noisy to whip up our fighting hate to a high pitch.

But I since have heard what American troops have done. American troops have committed acts in many countries of the world that are as ugly as the acts the Germans did. The Americans get by with it by saying those are only individual actions and are not the government policy. But when push comes to shove, Lieutenant Calley gets treated with kid gloves. He is almost a hero.

The people need to hear shocking things. They have to understand shocking things that are hard to tell them. The main source of information about those shocking things in this country is the Left, because they are some of the only ones who have kept the records. You have to be some kind of historian, or have more special knowledge than ordinary citizens have, to be able to understand that we sent the army out against the miners, and we sent the army out against the Okies. We sent the army out against the farmers who marched on Washington in the Whiskey Rebellion. We have done it a multitude of times.

There are whole huge outfits like Pinkerton who exist as a big company these days because they made so much money furnishing strikebreakers, furnishing private armies for the robber barons and the railroad barons.

The way the government was built, where the people vote to elect representatives, is not happening. The idea that the people vote to elect their representatives has been stripped of everything that made it potent, and trimmed down to the barest minimum compliance with the idea that the people vote and are represented. The Electoral College, in combination with television's stranglehold on opinion, in combination with the fact that the secret to heavy media is money, effectively stops any non-Establishment candidates from having a chance. And all the candidates we are presented with are either from the Establishment already or have enough money to be able to buy their way in at will.

Politics has become a matter of an adversary system that is almost exactly like the adversary system of the courtroom, where the actual issues of the question are buried in the form; and the form has grown and taken over the entire question. In the courtroom, everybody knows that the best lawyer is probably going to win, regardless of the guilt or innocence of the parties concerned; that people who are very guilty get off on absurd technicalities, if they have a good enough lawyer; and people who are not very guilty at all draw heavy life sentences if they don't have a very good lawyer.

At the same time, part of my heart was painted by Norman Rockwell.

One of the misconceptions of youth is that every gain in the liberty of the people will remain as a gain in the liberty forever. This attitude has caused the loss of freedom in many cultures at many times. The designers of the Constitution were people who felt oppressed by the law of King George and the monarchy of England and the other European countries. They tried to design a document that would protect their freedom. It is largely forgotten that Patrick Henry, of "Give me liberty or give me death" fame, did not attend the constitutional convention, and was actually an anarchist who would have preferred that the new nation of the United

States be allowed to grow a while longer before codifying the protection of its freedoms into a constitution. There is much to be said for his ideas. Here, in 1981, what we call the guarantees of the Constitution amount to the bare minimum of the protection that was envisaged by the writers. They tried to protect us. The message down through time of the Ninth Amendment to the Constitution is very clear:

That certain rights are herein enumerated shall not be construed to disparage or deny other rights which are retained by the people. Those rights are in severe jeopardy, from the attitude of the Supreme Court and the legislature who look at the Constitution as a bare minimum, not as a signpost pointing the direction of liberty for succeeding generations. No trace remains of Jefferson's dictum that every generation has the right to create its own form of government.

The Constitution, the laws concerning the giving of evidence, trials, punishments, were all designed to create a certain balance between the individual and the state so that the individual, in recognition of his small and weak political stature, compared to the might of the state, was given individual powers and privileges to render the dangers of trial more fair. Now, further down the line, the interpretations of those laws fall under attack from the Chief Justice of the Supreme Court himself, who travels the country and tells the world that we are too soft on the convicts, too easy on the criminals. Warren Burger was absolutely offended that someone, yet convicted, would continue to write writs to the Supreme Court, scratching and trying through a loophole in the law to obtain their freedom. And why should they not? The law is made of loopholes, a tissue of loopholes put together by the adversary system.

Arms of the government which were not powerful when our government was put together have since become powerful, and the government hasn't created machinery to balance them. If there are undelegated powers in a system, the power brokers will pull out of the systems with the delegated powers, and will put all of their value in the system with the undelegated powers.

Citizens need protection from the law. Citizens need protection from lawyers, who are not "our friends", but Officers of the Court who have a legislated higher social position than both complainants and defendants. The very delicate balance, between the individual and the state, has been greatly changed in the two hundred years of our country's existence. The original legal framers included a statute of limitations, in recognition that people change— that someone who had done something in the past and then kept himself clean and decent for a period of time, usually considered seven years, would outrun the statute of limitations; and whatever they had done would be written off in recognition that in seven years a new person could have emerged.

At the same time as the statute of time limitations, there existed another safety of the people, which was not written down because it was never considered that it would be necessary to write down such a thing. But it was always known that it was a big world, and you could leave when you got in trouble. If you went to a new place and didn't cause trouble, you could be left alone, and you could start a new life. The most romantic phases of the history of America speak of the men who ran from the Civil War, both as dischargees and deserters, who went to the West: pickpockets from New York, forgers from Cleveland, card sharks from New Jersey, all went to the West, to the territories, to make a new life. It was considered impolite to press a westerner on his history or his family, some of which was quite romantic. Doc Holliday, the dentist gunfighter, son of an English family that sent him a check by the month, to be certain that he didn't return to England: Doc Holliday was a remittance man. It was known that many people in the opening of the West were on the run, and there was even a song:

What was your name in the States?
Was it Johnson or Miller or Bates?

It was not a written-down right, that one could leave. But

111

in the real world, it existed as an alternative, and was one of the places where the system had enough slack to work.

The statute of space limitation. Nobody knew we had it. But as the space between the big cities got filled up with middle-sized cities, and the space between the middle-sized cities got filled up with towns, and the space between the towns got filled up with villages, and the leftover space became factories or forests or farmland, we used up our extra room. As people traveled from state to state, crossing the continent in three or four days on the freeway system, the states began to standardize the laws, so traffic and crime statutes stayed the same from state to state. The FBI asked for power to chase bank robbers across state lines; taking of automobiles or women for immoral purposes became federal business as they crossed state lines. With the national fifty-five mile an hour speed limit, and the national drivers' license computer, it became possible to relate every traffic incident back to one's own home state. The statute of space limitation was lost, without ever having been identified. But it's a little less free to live here than it used to be, as a result.

In the same way that the national drivers' license computer was unthought of, the helicopter was not considered in our tradition of law. Is not flying helicopters over a country low enough to see and interfere and intercede in it the same as being on the ground? I think so. Flying over it at such an altitude that you can't determine what's going on down there, not bombing it or affecting it or doing anything to it, is flying over it. Creeping along above the ground in a helicopter, close enough to see and close enough to fire and close enough to intimidate, is the same as being on the ground, and it works the same way for search warrants. Helicopter presence inside the borders is presence in the country; and helicopter presence inside a piece of private property is presence inside that property, and should be protected against.

Factors that were considered negligible by the framers of the Constitution have become pivotal: the acquisition of roads, and energy. The Highway Department has powers to condemn and buy property unparalleled outside of an absolute monarchy. The power of the utilities, not regulated under the Constitution, to condemn property and overrun local landholders on questions of nuclear power plants or nuclear waste dumps, has a built-in reckless disregard for the rights of the people involved which has not been seen in an English speaking country since the time of the Magna Carta.

The simple impulse to the welfare of the people shown in the general policy of cooperation by government agencies with medical entities gives the medical doctor ruling elite a quasi-governmental power and immunity so strong that the majority of Americans assume that doctor's orders are the same as government orders; they assume they have no rights if they are ill. The lending of government power to every medical endeavor, regardless of its profit-making status or the amount of oppression that accrues to the people, makes medical authority stand out as one of the major oppressors of the current scene, once again unregulated by the Constitution, outside of the system of checks and balances, no recourse for the people. Any contest between the medical establishment and mere humans will be resolved on the side of "normal medical practice", which changes so radically from generation to generation as to have scant claim to normality on any basis.

During World War II, American citizens gave up many powers and rights of privacy and communication semi-voluntarily in the name of emergency powers, to help fight the Nazis. The emergency powers in the United States were in response to the emergency powers that Hitler had assumed in the light of *his* continuing emergency.

During Prohibition, the alcohol police were given stronger and stronger powers until they were virtually able to walk in with blazing guns. In the last days the raids of the Untouchables became really frantic; the biggest alcohol raids and the greatest still bustings and beer-joint bustings that went on were just before they finally decided to pack it in and legalize it again.

It's like that now with marijuana. They pull off the biggest

113

bust in history. (I've heard that so many times in the last ten years that I can't remember what it means anymore, because every bust you hear about is always the biggest.) It's an economy of billions of dollars. Entire countries say they do not want to stop growing it and exporting it, because it is their major cash crop. Colombia and Jamaica don't want to spray paraquat, and disagree with the U.S. government about it, because it is so much a part of the national economy.

At the same time, it is decriminalized to some degree in twenty-five states. More and more legislatures are developing reasonable attitudes about its use for chemotherapy patients or its use for glaucoma patients. At a grass-roots level, there is a very quiet changing of the law going on. If that continues, they are no longer going to be able to justify the amount of money they have socked into the marijuana campaign. It looks like it could become legalized. The pressure to tax it is becoming stronger and stronger. People are saying, *This is a flow. It should be taxed.* They'll still keep their narcs, and still keep busting homegrown that way. They talk supply-side economics in Washington, but they don't understand it over at the Drug Enforcement Agency. They keep driving the price up and up, and more and more people take more risk to get control of it, as long as the price goes higher and higher. The reason guns got involved in marijuana was from the nature of money, not from the nature of marijuana.

But once again, the special police chartered out by the government began to assume broader powers, special powers, special powers of search, special powers of phone tap, special powers of infiltration and undercover. Marking, but not culminating the trend, is the recent legislation to give the narcotics police access to federal troops inside the borders of the United States, which changed a law that had been in effect since 1847. Over a hundred years of law changed to give the drug police broader powers.

Beyond the drug police lie the new kind of police, the ones who have the potential to monitor every aspect of our life: the nuclear police. These are the most awesomely powerful police imaginable. They can follow their geiger counter anywhere it clicks. They can walk into your house and take your stove and toilet and bed, and send it away to a laboratory. They can take your body, regardless of any statements of the Constitution, any separation of powers, any checks and balances. The nuclear police can take your body, on their sayso that you're contaminated. It shatters the writ of *habeas corpus*. It gives not just governmental police, but company police the most awesome power over property and body that police have ever had in a supposedly representationally governed country.

They never give back the emergency powers. After you get used to them, they ask for more. As Joan Baez said as far back as the 'sixties, we are clearly becoming shock-proof, because more and more shocking things happen to us all the time. We accept that numbly which would have had us screaming in the streets ten years ago. And we are being prepared to accept even more.

There Is No Majority

"There is a little bit of politics in every breath you draw."
Judge D.D. Humphries
General Sessions Court
Lewis County, Tennessee

Since the 1950's, there has been an awareness that the United States contains what were referred to as "minorities." The word "minority" has been pushed and shoved around into Washington, D.C.-ese, and NBC-ese and CBS-, ABC-ese, until it can be used virtually as any part of speech one cares to: it has been used as a convenient marker on the board for so long that it truly has been forgotten what that marker represents. We talk about giving the minorities a break. But the way the system works is that any minority, in the eyes of a huge, megalithic government, can become easy to write off. This was clearly stated by Henry Kissinger, referring to people in Micronesia: "Who cares what they think? There's only 90,000 of them."

There are about two hundred fifty million people in the United States now, and now a minority twenty-some million are black; another minority of millions is Jewish; another minority is Indian; another minority is Chinese. People who live in white middle class neighborhoods where the street lights are bright enough and the water pressure is good enough and the electricity stays constant, are a minority, too.

In truth, the majority is a myth: there is no majority. The

Moral Majority is just another minority; and to have their programs inflicted on the greater body as if they were the majority and the greater body the minorities, is to look at each minority individually, rather than realizing that they all have the same problems. It is not unreasonable for the activist women to make allies with the activist blacks, the activist Jews, the activist Indians, the activist homosexuals.

Any group that can be recognized as a subgroup, any discernible subculture, has, by virtue of its discernibility, the protection of the Constitution. There is a subculture in this country of alternative-directed, ecologically minded, pacifistic, idealistic dreamers and strivers, not just from the immediate last generation, but from the last three or four generations. They are also a minority, and they deserve protection under the law. Any protection of less than everyone is insufficient. Any stance on the question of human rights less than the full-hearted openness exemplified by Eleanor Roosevelt's Declaration of Human Rights is contrary to the principles on which this country was founded and organized.

Single issue politics such as nuclear power won't do it. But one has to understand the effect on society of yet one more group which can override the guarantees of the Constitution, and to realize that the constitutional guarantees are being overridden by the very existence of these interest groups.

If the majority of the people of this state say it costs six dollars to get a driver's license, I'll pay six dollars to get a driver's license. If the majority of the people in the state say that kids aren't supposed to drink booze until they are eighteen, or twenty, or twenty-one, or whatever the state decides, it's all right with me. But when the state says, *this is going to affect your life, your children and your freedoms,* they have to prove to me why I should accept that. I don't just have to eat that like a one per cent increase in the school tax.

I am all in favor of majority rules to take care of the scenery. But there is a place where a majority is not enough. Not two-thirds, not three-quarters. What I am worried about in this country is that my right to be against the foreign

118

policy or the nuclear power policy is not respected by the government. They say, if we can scrape together by hook or crook enough people to get the man in office, then you have to eat whatever we want to do. If we go start a war with Russia in your name, then you have to die in it along with us. The real people of power who run things are not elected.

The elected officials are turned into complete cosmetic jobs: people who can get elected because of whatever accidental media power they happen to have, like from going to the moon or being a movie actor or having a famous "royal" name.

There is a kind of freedom of speech that is granted on Hyde Park Corner in London, where you can stand up on a soapbox and say whatever you want. Single tax, silver standard, free money, screw the Queen, whatnot. They promote that. Of course, nobody ever travels from a soapbox on the square to a position of power. Nobody ever expects that anyone ever will. It's not a vehicle for change; it's more like a whistle on the teakettle.

The right to effective protest assumes that it is effective, rather than institutionally ineffective.

The right of petition, if it has any meaning at all, must include that the wrong must be possible of remedy by the medium of protest, otherwise the protest and its right are only window dressing. It is unreasonable to require a majority concurrence for a redress of grievances. Far too often, it is the majority which is the source of the grievance; and an oppressed minority must have an effective voice. What limits have the majority as to what they can impose on the minority? I did not elect Alexander Haig. Nobody elected Alexander Haig. It is the worst kind of non-representation for people like Kissinger, Schlesinger, Haig or Meese to have heavy hands in the government.

We have lost the idea of majority rule. We are now electing media specialists who then choose rulers.

The Golden Horns

My Uncle Charlie, who has been a political activist—he helped organize the waterfront in San Francisco; he's always been on the side of the people—told me the story of the Golden Horns.

Once there was a kingdom so small that all of the citizens could fit in the king's courtyard. When there was an election, they called in all the citizens of the country to come and stand in the king's courtyard. The rich and the poor were all there, and it was said that this was a country with a fair system of government, because everyone could vote.

The King's Vizier came out and read the resolution to be voted on. He read,

"Be it resolved, that the poor people shall pay all of the taxes, and that the rich people shall pay none."

"All those in favor," he bellowed, "Raise your golden horns and blow." And all the rich people raised their golden horns and blew a long, powerful note.

The King's Vizier went on. "All those opposed," he said, "Raise your golden horns and blow."

Not a sound was heard; for the poor people had no golden horns.

The Media

In the communications medium, our free speech is carefully calculated so that one is not guaranteed redress; only exposure.

The media have become a *de facto* arm of the government. The media became a *de facto* arm of the government when they began to cover the United States better than the governmental communications did. The reason Nashville, Tennessee, is on the map is because the Grand Old Opry had a 50,000 watt clear channel station. The opinions of Minnie Pearl are better known in this country than the opinions of Franklin Delano Roosevelt. She had more time on the air than he did. Hardly anybody could start imitating Roosevelt to you right now; but almost anybody could imitate Minnie Pearl. That's the power of a 50,000 watt clear channel station, before television. Attitudes of the country were partly formed by the Grand Old Opry.

Along about the same time, Will Rogers was riding around in a Ford Model T with a typewriter, writing a column wherever he was, and sending it in by telegraph to the New York City office, where it would be printed and syndicated to four hundred newspapers. He was an early user of the media.

They say that Will Rogers had such a tremendous feel for the consensus of the people, and so much personal influence, that Congress would never seriously try to pass a bill that Will Rogers was against. He called the Mayor of New York "Jimmy."

His power through the media was such that he played before the crowned heads and ruling *juntas* of all the countries. They would ask for Will Rogers to come and speak. He came to the diplomatic dinners; and the contents of his monologue were usually the substance of the agreements which were to be made. Usually, what he said in the monologue was the United States' position. He was a *de facto* ambassador, a *de facto* member of the government. He had free ride privileges in United States Mail planes.

That was before television. He had to go around and make personal appearances everywhere—which was why he eventually became friends with Wiley Post, and they flew around together. He died in a crash with Wiley Post, on his way to a gig.

He had to go around and make all those personal appearances to back up the four hundred syndicated newspaper columns and all the movies he did, ranging from *A Connecticut Yankee in King Arthur's Court* through the *The Ziegfield Follies.* He never changed his head for the movie parts. Always the same hair cut, always the same face. And hat, usually. He would wear costume from the neck down, including armor for *Connecticut Yankee.* He did not disguise his face because he was not supposed to submerge himself; *he was the medium*, and he had to keep his medium-ness. It was an early case of the medium is the message.

Those are early ways in which the press came into being part of the government. Another example was the way in which foreign policy was formed during the period just preceding the Spanish-American War. The Hearst newspaper chain decided for us what we were going to do, that we were going to get in that war.

Now we have the television, combining the power of the printing press, the still camera, the movie camera, the sound camera, and the color sound camera with the telegraph and the wireless. It combines everything that came before it. It's the most powerful medium ever created outside of the mind of humankind itself.

A few years ago they began to worry about the power of

the press in the election. Was fast reporting beginning to lead the poll?

The press flexed its muscle visibly for everyone to see, in the countdown of the vote which would be the harbinger of the vote that would be the indicator of an impeachment for Nixon. I forget what the question even was; but I remember that there was a question, maybe only of procedure, requiring the Constitutional two-thirds to pass because of the nature of the question. Each day, the television ran a little box score in the corner of the news which said, 197 votes for such-and-such; 203 votes for issue such-and-such; 206; climbing day by day. I don't know if anyone said it out loud, but it was well known that that was the people who would go for an impeachment. As more evidence came out during the hearings, day by day, the number went up and up, until it got to where it was only one or two away, and the news began to run profiles of the various congressmen or senators who were possibly thinking of changing their ideas according to the information as it came out; and we were focussed down on the decision making process of the guy whose mind would be the one which would add up the vote which meant impeachment. Everybody knew when that mind changed, that Nixon was impeached. And that mind changed, and Nixon resigned. The House and Senate impeachment process was rendered superfluous by the network computers; and the media became direct government.

The ship of state was wallowing around and there were rumors that Alexander Haig was running the country by disobeying Nixon's direct orders for the good of everyone. The cover of one of the national newsmagazines showed Walter Cronkite on his yacht, tan, healthy and honest, holding on to the wheel. It was the ship of state, and everybody knew that Walter was really the President. The ship of state was safe because Walter was at the wheel.

We sailed through with Walter for a little while before they got a government again. The media had become so *de facto* governmental, Woodward and Bernstein should have been congressmen. It would have been more honorable for this country if Woodward and Bernstein *had* been congressmen, if there had been any congressmen honest enough to blow the whistle on what many of them knew was going on. In a sense, Woodward and Bernstein *were* congressmen: they were the representatives of the people.

The media is a randomizing influence right now. They give you fiction in the news, and they give you news in the fiction. There is currently a war in television between the owners and the newsrooms on the one side, and the writers and the creative people on the other side. The writers, the actors and the creative people are putting out bad word on the right wing. There are right-wing villains showing up on all the sitcoms.

At the other end, Max Robinson gets in trouble for saying the reason he didn't get to go to the inauguration was because he was black. He got into a lot of trouble with ABC over that. He lectures at Smith College and says,

"I know my lecture is going back to the fourth floor at ABC where they are going to check out all this noise I've been making, and somebody is going to say,

" 'What are we going to do about that nigger?' "

That was in *TV Guide*.

He took off Martin Luther King's anniversary, and they said it was the wrong message for the network to send. He said,

"You take your holidays; I'll take mine."

I've done a lot of talking about the media and the media barons and princes; but I have to say that there are some of them who are very good. Bill Moyers is one of the very best. Bill Moyers is a teacher. He doesn't just exploit the issue of the moment, but he adds to the understanding of the issue of the moment, in one of the fairest ways on television. I even consider Bill Moyers to be a *spiritual* teacher. His religious background includes dropping out of being a minister. Although he dropped out, he had an idealistic vision of how fair and truthful one ought to be; and he tries to live that whether he is a preacher or not. I hope people like him get to stay on the tube and make it worthwhile.

The battle of thought in the media doesn't reflect reality; it is competing statements about reality. There's always a little race to keep the laws caught up with the swindles, and the swindles trying to stay ahead of the law. But the smart money bets on the place where the real power flows, not last year's empty form. That's why we have a movie actor for President. The real power obviously lies somewhere else.

The most blatant example of television governing instead of reporting that has happened to us lately was in the election of Ronald Reagan, where Jimmy Carter listened to his computer projections, and the advance polls were made public and were no longer advance. An advance poll that is made public and is no longer advance is then a self-fulfilling prophecy. Because of the time zones and the media reporting their projections the people in California were handed dead issues and dead ducks to vote for. The interaction of Jimmy Carter and the media robbed them of their sayso.

I believe in a free press; I would like the complaint I make to be understood in the context that I am in favor of a free press.

I experience censorship. The kind of thing I can talk about is severely restricted. It is assumed that I have a specialty, which is being a hippy. I experience censorship regularly on that basis; and I know that anyone else in a position similar to mine also experiences that same censorship. The news that goes out on the television into that half hour has to be combed and filtered and winnowed down and siphoned off and evaporated until it is such a thin mixture and so little of it compared to the number of things that actually went on that day, as to give a simplistic view of the world. An individual so simple-minded would be commitable, for not being smart enough to take care of himself.

A way the technology could help out would be if the phenomenon of the superstation could become common. We exist in slavery to the networks. The networks are monoliths, and the thing about a monolith is that somewhere there is a place you can grab it, and move the whole thing, because it's one chunk. So you look around until you find whatever you can grab that moves the whole thing. Is it Freddie Silverman? Is it General Sarnoff? Is it the advertisers? Somewhere in there, there is a handle. And people know where that handle is, and have their hand firmly on it. *The news we get does not offend the hand that holds that handle.*

It is even a scandal that the most important stuff is reduced to the public broadcasting system, because everybody knows that hardly anyone watches it. It's the quickest way to squelch something, to keep everybody from knowing about it: stick it on the public broadcast system.

The remedy for that is a portapack in every house. Everyone should be a producer of television as well as a consumer of it. If you're only a consumer of it, it will truly rot your mind. But if you can be a producer of it as well, if you understand how it is built and what is being said, it becomes a broad lake on which you can sail your paper boats, and they can sail as good as anyone else's paper boats.

It could become a medium for the people. Accidentally, something gets said on television once in a while. It's why one bothers to keep on watching.

I don't want to limit the investigative powers of the press. I don't want the press to lose its sources by being forced to divulge its sources of information. But I think that when an individual faces the press, it should be recognized that, in the same way in which when an individual faces the government, there is a great disparity in size, power, and experience in the arena.

I see regularly, and experience regularly, that a television interviewer can ask you questions that the judge would not allow the prosecutor to ask in a court of law, questions that if an FBI agent stood up and said in a court of law, the judge would hold him in contempt if he didn't shut up and stop immediately. A television reporter can put you out live to forty million people, with a magnified closeup of every pore of your skin. I maintain that when that camera's on you, you're under oath; and the people who ask you questions when you're on camera should respect that. I wouldn't care to see any legislation about any of this. I just think that anybody smart who faces the media ought to understand that for themselves. It's a new territory, and you have to take the freedom that belongs with that territory for yourself. Some day, the relationships between television and the individual will be established.

The power of the media is so huge that people are accidentally ennobled and sainted by touching that power. People who are announcers who have only said,

"Here's Johnny", or

"Buy this!" or

"And now this message," or

"The time is 7:30," or

"Tune in next week," have become powerful, well-known for being well-known.

This was a rare phenomenon when we first noticed it happening. Now it's become a whole genre. It relates a little bit to Andy Warhol who says that some day everybody will be famous for fifteen minutes.

People step into the Fame Game machine on the grounds that they have qualities that will make them go far. Farrah Fawcett or Susan Anton step into the spotlight of the Fame Game projector, and it says,

Presenting...Susan...Anton!!!

And she's there.

She's a medium singer, medium actress, all that. But she's striking looking. They found that content doesn't go too far; but images almost imprint.

And then, it suddenly becomes relevant, what does Farrah Fawcett brush her teeth with? Because among the factors that got Farrah Fawcett famous was her teeth, and her smile. So the way she cares for those teeth and that smile is relevant to the amount of money she makes and how well known she is, and therefore how much power she has as a media star.

So if someone asks and Farrah Fawcett says,

"I use Sudsadent,"

other young starlets, or girls who are not even starlets, just young girls who want to look nice like Farrah Fawcett, will

129

be thought to be interested in buying that toothpaste.

In contrast to that, we have Mother Teresa, whose teeth, as I recollect, may not be her own. But nobody cares what she brushes them with anyway, because she is not famous for the dental quality of her smile, or for being famous. She is famous for actions she has performed that are of sufficient preciousness and rarity as to be worthy of telling around the world.

Therefore, these are extreme ends of the Fame Game, but they are interesting parameters to use. You can have someone who is suspect of being a Fame Game player while actually pretending to be a political player, such as Ronald Reagan. Something I have not seen in any critical literature of late, but which may be noticed is that Ronald Reagan is the target of a lot of rather cutesy, kinky Hollywoodsy humor that none of our other Presidents has been subjected to. That's because he is suspected of being a Fame Game player; and it is open season on Fame Game players. If they make a mistake in the Fame Game, they're not supposed to get to go past GO and collect two hundred thousand dollars tax-free.

A reporter's style of interview toward a subject will change, according to his conscious, unconscious or subconscious perception of them as a Fame Game player. If he has any perception of them as a Fame Game player, his interview will not be supportive.

Malcolm Muggeridge is famous for having called the Queen of England such vile names as to be heard around the world. No tolerance for Fame Game players has old Malcolm. But when he did an interview with Mother Teresa, he called it *Something Beautiful for God,* and he did the very best job he could, because he had the grace to recognize that she was in no way a Fame Game player—media wise, media conscious, smart, hip, clever, but not a Fame Game player.

Johnny Carson treats Jerry Brown like a Fame Game player. Johnny is one of the scorekeepers in the Fame Game.

Television has become so much a creature of feedback, following the cause and effect of its demographic ratings, that it will do anything to get the numbers up, including telling deliberate lies. One of the things we got to see during the 'seventies was the widespread invention and use of the crockumentary. The crockumentary is privy to the secrets of the technical studio—special effects, film flown in from the far corners of the world, a library of tape and film going back decades, professional quality announcers—the exact same machine that brings you the Viet Nam war or the Watergate hearings brings you a documentary on the sasquatch, with a disclaimer shown on the screen for about a tenth of a second that says that "while the majority of scientific opinion maintains that there is no such thing as a sasquatch, this crockumentary is nonetheless prepared for the express purpose of making money."

Then it shows a footprint in one territory spliced in with a piece of acting of a lady running out of a house and screaming, spliced in with a statement by someone who thought they saw a sasquatch, spliced in with sensitive and touching footage of children dressed up as sasquatches playing in a creek through a fuzzy filter shot through the leaves a la European art style, all put together with the idea that maybe there is a sasquatch. But what is being shown on the screen, and the interaction between the words and the layout and the pictures says that there *is* a sasquatch, and a lie is put out on the minds of millions and millions of people, for the sake of ratings. That is where television really sins.

One of television's worst is the crockumentary which suggests that, because axolotl is a southern Mexican Indian word for salamander, that spacemen landed in the Yucatan which has unexplained markings in the swamp and salamanders, in order to reclone the space crew because salamanders are good at cloning, spliced in with latest footage of actual cloning of real salamanders in real laboratory. Bad for the mind of humankind.

This is a symptom of the machine running wild on feedback, doing anything it takes to get the Nielsens.

As a general principle, the supersession is evidence of the decadence of a form. Consider the evolution of jazz. There were guys who learned jazz where it first came from, and there were the jazz giants—Louis Armstrong, W. C. Handy and the heavy old names. Then, through the recording system—again the media prejudicing the situation—and radio, these guys became hooked into a genre, instead of just being a bunch of individual musicians doing their thing. Once they were hooked into a genre, then they could be pulled together to play supersessions. Then you had the guys who had been the bandleaders of the hottest bands all getting together into a band made out of the hot band leaders. This is a supersession.

Jazz fell to such a low ebb after its supersession phase, that rock and roll benefits were held to give money to the San Francisco jazz club, the Both/And, to help keep it alive, because there wasn't enough interest in jazz to keep the club going for the form.

When the rock and rollers distinguished themselves, then they started having supersessions—the guys from the hot bands jamming together; evidence of the decadence of the form.

When I first heard rock and roll, I thought,

"Here's guys who have the guts to take the crescendo of a Beethoven ending and use it for a beginning and go all the way through with it, and shatter all those old forms."

Then they became a form, and then they started having supersessions, and their form started to decay.

In television, we have a great example of the decadence of a form; the form we are experiencing the decay of is the short story. The short story is not an accident in the mind. The study of the short story is a form of the study of psychology; the anecdote is the way in which the mind stores information. A short story that carries a piece of information in it is its own filing system. Short stories come out nicely by subject.

I was an old science fiction reader. I read all the science fiction short stories. Then I branched out into straight short story. I went to college and was an English major. I did short stories. I studied the novel. I studied American literature, English literature, world literature. I have seen the permutations of the short story come through—to the degree that now I understand where my writing teachers were at when they told me I didn't yet have the breadth to recognize all the permutations of the short story as soon as I saw them.

On television, if you take a story like *Star Trek*, the series will first use up its thirteen weeks of originally written pilot stories. Then it will start asking other writers to write stories for it. Then it will start stripping the science fiction short story books, with and without permission and copyright infringement—sometimes actually using old classic stories and modifying for television, other times just pulling the guts out of old stories and not even saying where they got it from, until by the time it has run a certain number of episodes, it has done all the permutations of the short story in that medium; and the series goes dead.

They have tried various things in order to try to hype the series back to life when it goes dead. One offers another example of the decay of the form. In classical Greek short story form—although they never called it that—there is the scenery, the environment. When it happened, how it happened, no anachronisms, no mixing of places, you have a continuity of place and time that keys to reality sufficiently to make the story interesting to someone who has to live in reality. The *verities*, they called them.

The Six Million Dollar Man had run through the short story genre and the science fiction genre as *Star Trek* did before it. The only thing in *The Six Million Dollar Man* that was unusual was the bionic man himself. It's twentieth century United States, with the Russians and the Americans, the Democrats and Republicans—different names, OSI instead of CIA, but very recognizable. The only gimmick is the bionic man. This places him in the same relationship to the rest of the world that coming from the planet Krypton did for Superman.

You could tell when they broke the form. In one show, not only did the Bionic Man find a sasquatch, which made something other in the world than the bionic man who was that powerful—breaking the forms of the world—but the sasquatch turns out to be an android sasquatch built by

133

beings from outer space, and we have gone into wild free-flowing science fiction with creatures from another universe, with different laws of physics.

Well, this was exciting for a couple or three episodes, but it was burning the background like firewood. It burned the verities out in a very few episodes, and the Bionic Man went irretrievably dead. They had burnt the realities out until it didn't matter what it was any more because it was up for grabs.

When it gets where it doesn't matter what's on television, then it won't matter what's on television.

Modern television has evolved so fast in the last ten years that the mind rejects pre-television movies for their slow and boring delivery of information. The intrinsic qualities of television, the way in which it is edited at the push of a button rather than through a laboratory process like film, and the competitive nature of commercial television have combined to produce a giant teaching machine. Hyperactive schoolchildren who cannot read or write are sophisticated television critics.

Twenty years ago or more, experiments were done, chopping small segments out of sound tapes to see how much could be removed without the listener noticing he was being fed the information. Modern television editing shows more respect for the integrative powers of the mind than the previous media did. The last three minutes of *The Electric Horseman* had over 110 cuts. We use as dramatic devices speeds of cutting that would have been considered subliminal twenty-five or thirty years ago.

McLuhan is being borne out. The content of television is a previous form, which we are beginning to see through easily. We are still learning the new form.

Chapter XXII

This chapter is the chapter where we thought it would probably be better if we didn't mention the names of all the newspeople, audio, video and print, who have smoked dope with me and have blown my cover in their article or story, but not theirs.

The Walls

When I went into the penitentiary up in Nashville at the Walls we were put up in a room that was like a holding area. They had 120-130 prisoners in it. Civilians, your non-convict folks, don't really understand why they have all those separate cells in the pen. It's because some of the people in the pen are genuine bad-asses and you need to be protected from one another; and it was a scary thing to be up in a big room with 120 guys.

The first night we were there we saw a duel that looked like a gladiator duel. One guy had a dust pan and a mop handle. The other guy had a razor. They fought, and the winner shoved the loser's head in the toilet.

That night I tried to sleep. How in the world can anybody sleep in a place like this? I was hyper and keyed up by how dangerous and scary and strange it was in that big room. Guys were sitting up all night playing cards. I felt that the light bulb they were playing under pierced through my skin and that my skin had eyes. I had to cover myself with blankets, although it was hot, to try to keep that light from touching my skin because it was so intense to be that keyed up for that long. Didn't really sleep hardly. The next night I couldn't understand how people could sleep in such an environment. The third night I began to understand how people could sleep in that environment. The third night I was tired enough and run down enough and I had enough fatigue toxins and enough heavy emotion toxins running through my body that my body needed to sleep and I went to sleep.

That was the level of consciousness, short three days of sleep, it took to match speeds with the other people there, all of whom were short three days of sleep, too. Now, you know when you're overrun and stay up all night the next day you're not as sharp. Even though along about 9 o'clock in the morning you can forget about sleep, and you think,

"Hot dog! I can stay up the rest of the day," and you feel all right, but you ain't quite as sharp. The second day you're not very sharp at all. By the third day you begin to stumble around a little. It's a level of consciousness. What kind of consciousness have you got after you've been awake two or three days? What are you able to maintain?

Being a vegetarian in the penitentiary was an experience. The first time it came time for chow call, I went to the sergeant who was our immediate guard, and said,

"I'm a vegetarian, and I want to know how I should go about getting chow."

Sergeant Nunnally looked a little puzzled and annoyed by my request; then he smiled and said, "You can just go on over to the mess hall, and line up with the Black Muslims."

I walked over to the mess hall to line up with the Black Muslims, expecting to step into a chow line. When I found the Black Muslims, they were standing at attention in three ranks with a platoon commander.

I didn't know what else to do, so I went up to the platoon commander and said,

"Sergeant Nunnally said that because I was a vegetarian, I was supposed to line up with you guys."

He looked at me and said, in a cold, dead level voice,

"Someone-has-been-sending-you-up."

I saw there was no further conversation possible at that time. I went back to Sergeant Nunnally to tell him I really couldn't do that.

The next time I went to the chow hall, I watched the Black Muslims enter the chow hall, and understood even more fully how foolish and dangerous it would have been. The Muslims entered the chow hall in ranks at attention, sat quietly, orderly and neatly at the tables; and when their head man came in, they gave to him the respect that was so obviously lacking when they spoke to the guards. One stood behind his chair and pulled his chair out; one helped him off with his coat; one cleared the table to make room for his tray. They sent word by their deed they were not uncivilized, that to one for whom they had respect, much respect was given, and for those who did not receive respect, it was deliberate.

We were transferred shortly after that from the holding cell where a hundred twenty of us were kept in one room to a four-man cell, with my three community-mates who went to prison with me. All the hippies were put together in one cell; it was easier to keep track of them.

I wrote a letter to the warden about being a vegetarian. I knew that eventually recognition would be taken that I was a vegetarian. Sure enough, my answer from the warden was not a comment on my letter or a statement about my letter, but merely a permission slip to have free run of the chow hall and browse where I wished.

As we spent our time and got to know the other prisoners, black and white, and guards, they realized that we were serious about our ways. While standing in the chow line, I felt a shoulder thrown against my back in a not-unfriendly fashion. I looked over my shoulder and saw that same tall platoon commander of the Black Muslim platoon. He leaned over my shoulder, indicated a pot of white beans, and said,

"Them beans is clean, brother," and recognized my dietary preference as a moral issue, as was his.

Chief Joe Casey talks about how the prisons have it so nice. They have a salad bar—well, a salad bar just means you get to pick what you want instead of having it stuffed on your plate. Otherwise, you have to eat something anyway, and salad is one of the things they give you to eat. He says they have honor dorms. I don't know if Chief Joe Casey would live in the honor dorm. The honor dorm is the old holding cells for the electric chair.

It's a small, low building with a large transformer on the roof, with six or eight cells in it. When capital punishment was outlawed, those cells were made into the honor dorm, where you could lock yourself in. One thing you don't want if you're in the penitentiary, is a cell with a door that doesn't lock. You have to be locked in for safety. Those guys could lock themselves in their own cells. They weren't going anywhere. They were allowed to paint the bars. They were allowed to hang cloth on the walls of the cells that used to be the holding cells for the electric chair. Cheery little place, called the Honor Dorm, Unit Six.

We met visitors in the Visitors' Room at the Walls. Those visitors never knew, or didn't understand, that that clean and well-lighted Visitors' Room, where you could look but not touch your love, was suspended in the midst of a giant machine; to go to that little room, we walked through a cellblock several stories high of cages, and climbed a long metal ladder to a door set three stories high in a wall. As you climbed the long metal ladder past the front of those cell blocks, people jeered and screamed.

Then you stepped into a small room, where you took off every article of clothes and left it hanging on the wall, and walked to the next room in a small hallway carrying your socks and your underwear in your hand.

At a small glass window, your socks and underwear were given for inspection to a guard for whom I always felt compassion—rummaging around among the footstinks and nicotine stains for something small and portable.

Then we stood over a mirror so the guard could see up our rectum without bending over, and spread wide our mouth and rolled our tongues.

When our inspection was complete, we were allowed to go to the next room, where we picked up the clean, bright, blue, soft, ironed, creased uniform: a jumpsuit, with our own socks and shoes and our own underwear, and were permitted to go into the next room looking clean and neat, with no hint of the sometimes ill-fitting and ragged clothes that we had left in the other room.

I was in the Visitors' Room when Tom Snyder, who was doing a documentary at the Walls, asked if I would be one of the prisoners he would interview. I said, "Sure," and walked over to a low table with Snyder and discussed the kind of thing we might say.

I suddenly noticed a looming presence standing, almost touching my elbow as I sat in a low chair. I looked up into the face of the Commissioner of Corrections. He said,

"Good day. I am the Commissioner of Corrections. I just wanted to introduce myself to you before you had your interview."

I caught eyes with Snyder, and we knew I was getting my instructions about, *watch your mouth, be careful what you say.*

I tried to talk, in that shiny lit-up room, about what it was like just on the other side of the wall, in the great, grey, man-keeping machine.

People on the outside don't really realize that those walls are actually pretty transparent to social movements that pass through. When the fad and the craze across the United States and on the campuses and in the fraternities was to streak, we in the penitentiary knew about streaking, too. We had our champion streaker, Fat Man.

The day Fat Man streaked marked an educational day for me. As Fat Man left one corner of the exercise yard, two hundred and fifty pounds, about five-foot-eight, and streaked, or waddled, across to the other side, the cons cheered and whistled and stomped and shouted encouragement: *Get it, Fat Man!*

Then the guards came and grabbed Fat Man for being nude in the exercise yard. They were going to bust him and take him down to the hole for his breach of the rules.

But a joke is a joke, and a good joke deserves support. So felt the cons, and they surrounded Fat Man and the guards who were going to take him with three hundred serious convicts. Not your college students in caught selling a lid to a nark. Not your drunk driver in for too many drunk drivings. But your serious residents, citizens of the subculture of the penitentiary, surrounded Fat Man and the guards, and said,

141

"It was a good joke. Let it lay as a joke. Leave it alone."

It was as beautiful and spontaneous a political demonstration as ever happened. And the guards immediately backed down.

Down the line, as word travels in the penitentiary, more light was shed on Fat Man's Great Streak. We found he had been challenged to the event with a prize of forty dollars, which he collected for his inspired and courageous streak.

There was a fair amount of controversy among the prisoners about whether Fat Man's streak had been an obscene act or not, inasmuch as Fat Man was so fat that you couldn't see anything, anyway.

A little piece of sovereignty was expressed right there, and something was kept in proportion by the will of the people. Even in the most degraded condition, you can still express sovereignty.

Mahatma Gandhi said that pacifism is very active and dynamic.

The dining hall in the penitentiary is a great low-ceilinged room which I am told was much improved from previous days when there used to be a machine gun in the corner, with the seats all fastened to one spring so they would all spring up together and slam back as the convicts stood up—but the penitentiary had somewhat improved, and there was a place to get salads, you were allowed to finish your meals.

I had just got my tray, going through the line, and was partly through my meal when several men came over from other tables in the room, and stood around my table and began to talk to me, and ask me questions about why I was in the penitentiary and what I was doing there, wondering why someone who seemed as harmless and as honest as I should be in the pen. While they were talking to me, a group of guards noticed that there were several men standing around my table, talking to me. They didn't want to leave the situation, to their mind, deteriorating, with people walking around the chow hall instead of sitting carefully in their seats, but they didn't want to draw attention to what was causing their problem. So, in an ill-conceived notion, they said our line of tables was finished eating, and we could get up and go.

At the beginning of the line of tables, where I was sitting, the men *were* almost finished eating; but down at the other end, many of them had just sat down with their trays, and their trays were pretty full. But the guards had ordered that line of tables to be cleared, and those men had to get up and scrape those trays, some of them almost full, into the garbage can, and leave.

I felt that a great injustice had been done. I felt disturbed that those men lost that meal over me; I felt that the guards had been cowardly in not speaking what the real problem was and clearing a whole line of tables instead; and I resolved to tell the guards what I thought.

I loitered behind a pillar until the chow hall was empty and all the prisoners had returned to their cells. Finally, there was nobody left in the chow hall but me and six or eight guards who were catching a cigarette over in the corner.

I walked over to where the guards were, and I began to tell them that it was wrong, and unjust, that they had done a wrong thing to those men, that it was no way to run a penitentiary, that it was completely unfair. I began to give them hell. I didn't curse them; I didn't call them any obscene names. I just told them that what they had done was wrong; that I could tell it was wrong; that everyone knew it was wrong. And in the situation I could see how being in the position of clearly having the right was so strong that I could stand and tell six or eight mace-armed guards where they were at, and there was nothing they could do about it; and they did nothing about it.

I noticed that one of them seemed a little affected by what I had said, and I made sure that I would give him a piece of literature later on and try to make a friend of him. I saw that, just like Mahatma Gandhi said, if you're right, a lot of times there is nothing they can do about it. Nothing can be said. If you're right, you get to speak your piece.

A penitentiary name is kind of like a CB handle; it

somehow expresses something about you that might not get expressed by the one your mother gave you.

One of my favorite handles belonged to a tall, blond young man who was enough of a trustee that he was allowed to go down the aisleways and hallways of the cellblock sweeping up. As he swept along, he ran his rather long neck out in front of him as he leaned against the broom, and many people called him "the Buzzard."

Buzzard came sweeping down the rock, past a cell of blacks who said,

"Hey Buzzard! Come over here a minute, Buzzard."

And Buzzard turned and said,

"If you must call me Buzzard, you must call me *Mr.* Buzzard."

And they said, "Okay. Mister Buzzard Double X. We'll make you an honorary Muslim. Mister Buzzard Double X."

And he became Buzzard Double X, the only white man with a Double X name I ever met.

They said about Buzzard Double X that you had to watch him. I suppose that might be because of the story that circulated, that he frequently sold aspirins dotted with a magic marker pen to new prisoners for LSD. As the fellow said who told me the story,

"That ol' Buzzard's about half-slick."

Justice Burger complains because the prisoners, even after they were arrested and tried and convicted and went to jail, would still not stop their—and he used this word—their *assault* on the Supreme Court of the United States by the writing of writs. Even in jail for their crimes, they have not repented, but still write writs.

I was glad to hear that. It was a convict, the prisoners told me, who started the law library in the Walls at Nashville. He was a man who wrote writs and wrote writs. He wrote writs until they threw him in solitary for writing writs. And from solitary confinement, he wrote a writ on toilet paper, and sent it out. And it scored, and bought him his freedom.

When he left, he left his books for the law library at the Walls, in case somebody else could write a writ. He wrote

144

writs about writing writs until they locked him up for writing writs, and he wrote a writ that worked.

Nobody better quit writing them writs.

I used to read spiritual books, some of which said that the crime you couldn't recover from was taking a life. It put you outside the pale, somehow, of humanity. But I was in the penitentiary with a lot of different kinds of people, and some of them had done killings. Some of them had done killings that were so ugly and so repulsive and so sick that I almost didn't know how I could relate to those people. But as I stayed in the pen, I began to realize that those were people, too. They were human beings. I found myself sitting and having dinner several evenings with a guy who told me that he hadn't actually killed anyone, but he had done a robbery and shot up some people. He said,

"I'll tell you what got me my ninety-nine years, was when a teenage boy came in paralyzed from the waist down in a wheelchair, and pointed at me and said, 'That man shot me down like a dog.' I got my ninety-nine years right then."

There was another prisoner there called Madame Razor Blade, who was supposed to have done something unspeakable to his family—dismembered them, perhaps, and left them in the trunk of a car. He dressed as close to a woman as he could, within the limits of the penitentiary garb, and he had his act down pretty good. He wore a bright pink washcloth tucked in his collar like a scarf, and he wore his pants pulled as high as he could pull them, and belted his belt as tight as he could, until it made a little waist, and an imitation of the round bottom of a woman. He had his moves down pretty cold. He moved like a woman. He combed his hair in a hairdo that was a pretty good imitation of a standard Tennessee lady's beehive, bubble-hair hairdo.

When you caught Razor Blade out of the corner of your eye, and saw his moves, it made you snap your neck and say,

"What? Is there a woman here in the joint?"

And when you got your head turned and saw what it was you snapped for, Razor Blade would be there, and he would smile and look at you with that look that said, just as clear as anything,

"Got you again, didn't I?"

Even at that, the other prisoners in the pen didn't like to see the guards bust into Razor Blade's cell and take away all his pretty stuff. They thought it was wrong to take away from Razor Blade whatever little it was that he had.

I watched Razor Blade from a distance until one day, standing in the chow line, picking up a cup of fruit juice out of the cooler, I found myself face to face with Madame Razor Blade, who looked at me, and the telepathy was as clear as a bell.

Without ever opening his mouth, just from eye to eye, he said,

You say you love people. You say that everybody's worth something. You say you believe in being kind. Are you going to recognize me as a human being? Are you going to look in my eyes and say hello to me as a human being? Or are you going to turn your back on me because of what I did?

I could not turn my back on him. I had to look him in the eye and acknowledge his presence in the world and say,

"Howdy," which is to say, "How do ye?" and recognize his humanity.

Something changed in me then, and I knew I could not be exactly the same way I was, even about someone who had taken a life.

Sergeant Fury's drag, although I didn't recognize it at first, was as extreme as Madame Razor Blade's. I didn't even recognize Sergeant Fury's drag for drag at first. I knew there was something about it, the shaved head, prison hat starched up crisp like an army hat, sleeves torn off, tunic, tight belt, combat boots, bloused pantlegs, some kind of a costume which I immediately nicknamed Sergeant Fury.

I watched Sergeant Fury, and I thought that he was at the other extreme, the other pole, from Madame Razor Blade. But then I realized that getting himself up like a French Foreign Legionnaire or a Marine Corps drill instructor was just as weird a thing to be doing inside the joint as getting yourself up like a lady was; it was just another kind of drag. Then I

146

just thought, *Sergeant Fury, Madame Razor Blade, both wearing drag.*

I was in jail before the Lynyrd Skynyrd crash, and their song, "Free Bird" was high on the charts. It's a funny kind of song. I don't really care for the vocals; I'm not really hot for songs about how I'm going to leave you again, baby. But the jam, with those three guitar players tumbling over each other faster than light, is one of the finest things in rock and roll.

We were in an eight foot by eight foot cell, and whenever "Free Bird" came on and cut from the vocals to the long jam, Wilbur would turn up the volume and we'd listen to it. One afternoon I was asleep, and "Free Bird" came on the radio. Wilbur turned it up, and I could hear that jam in my sleep.

I began to have a dream that I was escaping. I was running in my sock feet down long, smooth marble halls, laying over on the side on the corners like a fast-cornering motorcycle, clawing sideways like a cheetah in my sock feet across the smooth floors. Down the long hallways, hot and fast, with the "Free Bird" jam right on my heels.

When the bass player gave the signal to bring the jam around, I hit the door of the penitentiary and burst out the door, out into the outyard, where a great, grey elephant stood.

As I looked at the elephant, his belly shrank until it was emaciated, and his great ribcage hung down. His trunk shrank back into the muzzle of a gigantic greyhound, elephant sized.

When I woke, even though I woke in jail, I was high and happy, and felt good from the good energy of that fine jam, and the fine, fast, smooth run I had had down those hallways into that great shrinking elephant that turned into the greyhound that obviously symbolized The Farm's greyhound bus coming to pick me up someday.

I sat on a bench outside the counselor's office, waiting my turn to come in and talk to him, being very careful and watching who else was in the area; it was well-known that someone had been robbed while sitting on that bench recently, and hadn't even told the counselor when their time had come. This is indicative of how much the administration knows about what is going on.

When my turn came, the counselor was young and intelligent, and affected to understand me as a philosopher or flowerchild priest. We discussed not only as prescribed by the regulations my "drug problem", which was mandatory for all drug-related offenses, but began to examine my basic sanity and my attitudes as a founder of The Farm, our community.

He was fairly interesting and amusing for someone to talk to in the penitentiary; and I felt that if he had understood spiritual principles a little better he might have been able to realize more of his potential than he was on a purely materialistic, behavioral view of reality.

At some point he mentioned visiting The Farm. The Farm has a lot of visitors, thousands a year. I thought it would be all right. I told him it was okay with me if he wanted to go visit, he didn't need to do anything special, our gate wasn't that formal. All he needed to do was go down and ask for a tour, and they'd give him a tour.

The next word I heard of his activities was related to me by the Farm people on visiting day. He had come to The Farm gate, introduced himself as my counselor from the penitentiary, and began to throw his weight around at the gate, as though somehow by being in the penitentiary gave him special power or privilege on The Farm. I was somewhat amused at this report, as it showed my contention that he did not understand us or what we were doing.

As he got obnoxious and threatened and made faint, veiled threats of power and influence on his part, the gate crew reacted to him as they would to any person who came to The Farm and tried by aggression or power to impose themselves on the people. They turned him around and told him that he was not going to be welcome as a visitor after all. Fortunately, I was sent to a new counselor fairly soon.

Mr. P., from Columbia, was a fine man. He was our guard on Unit Five. He was a neat, tidy man, a gentle and well-educated southerner who looked at his job in corrections the way someone who's a social worker looks at their job. He showed that you don't have to live in San Francisco to be hip. He knew that folks generally enjoyed talking and rapping with the hippies, and he would frequently come down the cellblock and hit the lock on my door with the practiced moves of a real, professional turnkey, with a move so swift that you couldn't believe your door was open until you tried it and it moved. He let me out to go hang on the bars of other people's cages.

He had even more sense of humor than that. It wasn't just me that he sent out on the block to try to calm and soothe the other prisoners, but the tall, black drag queen in cell number four, whom he allowed out on the block to plait cornrows on everybody's head who wanted them. He saw that with a little humor and a little decency, things could even be made easier in a concrete cage.

Some of the most Constitution I ever saw during my time inside the walls was when King Kong was on duty. King Kong was a guard. He was huge—six-four or -five, a handsome black man. Good looking, intelligent, and a good hearted man who said that as far as convicts went, he didn't see race. Convicts told stories of King Kong. When several black guards took down a white prisoner and began to beat him, King Kong waded into the hassle like a hunter wading into his hunting dogs, grabbing them by the scruff of the neck and throwing them into the corners. And it was known that he would have rescued a black con or a white con equally. To someone like me, for whom 155 pounds is more of an ambition than my actual weight, I breathed a little deeper and a little easier when King Kong was around. When King Kong was on duty, the Constitution was in effect.

God Bless Mr. P. from Columbia. And Bigfoot. And King Kong and Mr. Bass. And the other honest people in the corrections system, because we need them really bad. We underpay our guards and wonder why they are not aware of the latest scientific and psychological developments. They barely have enough money to pay rent.

I crossed paths with several local celebrities in my time. W. T. Hardison was in for some kind of a bank swindle which I never understood. He was a humorous and intelligent man who, whenever he was asked what went with the supposed millions of dollars of swag, he always said,

"Ask my dog."

I saw W. T. on the street. Standing beside him was a small English terrier of some kind. I bent over and looked the dog seriously in the face, and queried,

"Where's the money?"

It didn't do me any good, any more than it had the reporters or the warden.

James Earl Ray was in at the same time as I was, but they had him in maximum security for his own protection.

The people in the penitentiary who were sad were not the strong, amusing people like W. T. Hardison or the long-timers; my heart wept for the ones they called the "punks". Not what you'd call a punk on the street. Not some tough kid in a leather jacket backing off humanity with the snarl and screech from an electric guitar. The punks were eighteen year-olds and occasional seventeen year-olds that some jury out in the county somewhere had seen fit to send to the penitentiary. They could be seen walking around the exercise yard with shaved heads when all the other prisoners had long hair. They wore ill-fitting clothes, and crept around in the corners trying to stay away from people. Because of their youth, because they were not fully grown and did not have a man's musculature to defend themselves with, they were sometimes the repeated victims of the prison homosexual rape.

I was once thrown into a cell with three young men. One was quiet and nondescript, and I can't remember him very well, because the other two were so stunning in their character types. One was about twenty-two, strong and well-built, six feet, maybe a hundred seventy-five pounds, with bright red hair and sunbleached yellow-blond eyebrows, a ruddy complexion—a handsome, beautiful young man in his prime. The other, with his shaved head and his saggy-bottomed pants, had been pushed as a punk so long that he had begun to play the role. The young man was so driven by his hormones that his eyes grew red like a bull. The shaved-headed boy rolled his t-shirt up in a simulacrum of a brassiere, and belly-danced while I sat in the corner and read comic books. Not what you would call "gay", but just pure prison lust.

I heard the red haired boy say,

"You just hammer them up alongside the head enough times and that old jaw opens."

The convicts say, *If you can't do the time, then don't do the crime.* Of all the possible failings catalogued in the penitentiary, the worst is to fall weak.

The reason I'm coming out of the penitentiary talking this way is not because I was damaged so much by it, because I after all am supposed to be a professional keep-it-together person. They would have been able to laugh and hoot and point quite a lot if I had rolled over and folded up in their old penitentiary, so I wasn't about to. But I had a lot going for me. I got to read spiritual books, and I got a lot of support. My family was not down on me and didn't hate me because of what I'd done. Nobody felt like I'd betrayed them. I didn't have any bad vibes coming from the Farm because of what I'd done. It was actually a burn for me to have to do the time since I'd been against planting it anyway, so I had optimum conditions going into it. So I'm not saying all this horrendous stuff in the nature of a complaint. But if a young person, eighteen years old, maybe, does something crazy, maybe drunk, maybe barely knows what he's doing, he can find himself slapped into a place that is outside the United States and as away from the protection of the Constitution as if it were on another planet.

The inside of penitentiaries do not belong to the world; they belong to hell. They have different ground rules. There is no order inside the penitentiary. There is a minimum of order imposed on it, and a maximum of infrastructure to keep order: cells and bars and special lights and electric eyes and guns and mace and uniformed guards and radio and all of that to create order, and there isn't any order. Standing in line and eating at the same time is not order.

The life that goes on, not for the people like me who just came in for a year, but for the people who are going to be there a long time and have to put together some kind of a life to live inside that place, is something else.

I am reminded of one guy I saw complaining to Sergeant Fury one time about a problem he had. The next time I saw him, several days later, he came walking by and he had on a prison shirt, sleeves torn off, and a picture of a beautiful, long-haired hippy boy on his back, with a very light downy mustache and little bits of golden curls along his cheekbones and long hair, a beautiful hippy boy. And he said to Sergeant Fury,

"You know that problem I was telling you about that I had? I ain't got no problem anymore. Everything's all right now."

What he was alluding to was that, through bribery or political power or some means or other, he had arranged to have someone transferred into his cell whom he could intimidate into being his submissive lover. So he didn't have a problem any more, because he had managed to get somebody in his cell that he could handle. He was going to live there for the rest of his life, and who was going to be in that cell with him was his wife, whether or not they had had some other life before that.

I'm not talking about the day trippers. It hurts them, and it damages their life. But for the people you just stick in there, fifty, sixty, seventy years is meaningless.

When they're fixing to let you out, they tell you,

"Hey, you're getting out today! It's time to pack your junk and kiss your punk."

"Drop your cocks and get your box."

A *shiv* used to be prison talk for a knife. But *shiv* isn't prison talk for a knife anymore, it's old fashioned. Prison talk for a knife is now a *shank*. I don't know whether that's the shank of a spoon, or like the steel shank out of a shoe; but somehow, it's a shank. They used to say that the prison love song was, *Shit on my dick or blood on my shank.* I know this is a little rough for public consumption, but I wanted you to know what you were doing when you send young people to the penitentiary, where you are sending them and what you are exposing them to. What did you think you would get back after exposing them to that?

Turney Center

When I used to live in the north or the west, I used to hear southerners complain that the northerners would come in and screw up race relations in ways where there had been some kind of an arrangement arrived at over the realities of living together over hundreds of years. In some places it had been worked out where it worked in a southern fashion. Not all the southern customs were bad. Some of the southern customs made it easier to live. I had heard of this sort of thing, but I had never experienced it until I saw the case of bringing in a Yankee from outside the state to become Commissioner of Corrections. That was one of those cases.

Mr. Charles Bass was Assistant Commissioner of Corrections when I went into the penitentiary—a strong, kind black man with a down-home manner of speech. For reasons that I learned as I went along, Mr. Bass had the trust of the prisoners. Mr. Bass was just the complete opposite of Mr. Luttrell, the Commissioner of Corrections. Mr. Luttrell cared for the welfare of the prisoners in the way that the manager of a farm cared for the welfare of the creatures of the farm—essentially decent, but not really in communication with his charges. Commissioner Bass was the one who made you know that there was some justice in the system.

I first saw Commissioner Bass when I was in the Walls in Unit Five. He was talking to some guys in the next cell. One of them said,

"Commissioner, I spent several months in the county jail, and now I'm up here in the penitentiary, and they told me they ain't going to give me my county time."

Commissioner Bass attracted my attention by the immediate and serious attention he paid to the young man's complaint. He took the convict's name and number and said,

"I'll find out about your county time for you."

He went away, and was back the next day. He had traced down the young man's county time, and told him he would get his county time. He had fixed that for that young man right then, in one day, expedited it, figured it out, and got it together for the young man, who happened to be white. Commissioner Bass never showed to me any preference for black or white prisoners.

I spoke with Commissioner Bass once or twice as he was dealing with the boys in the next cell—he, a little curious about me, I suppose, for being the hippy from the Farm, and me about him because he was the Assistant Commissioner of Corrections, a man of great power in the eyes of all the prisoners. Mr. Luttrell left; there was a new Commissioner of Corrections. Many people felt that Mr. Bass should have become Commissioner of Corrections; but as long as he stayed there as Assistant Commissioner and you could rely on his honesty and his integrity, it was felt that he guaranteed some of the justice in the system, and in a way that was not planned, but just worked out that way, helped guarantee the fairness for the large number of black prisoners in the penitentiary, and eased the racial tensions by his presence and his integrity.

I had cause to call on Commissioner Bass for help myself, one time. Not I exactly, but my family. I had been transferred to a Center for Youthful Offenders, although I was neither youthful nor, I felt, particularly offensive. More probably, it was done to get me away from the Nashville media. But I immediately found myself crossways with the penitentiary system.

There seemed to be a multiplicity of ways to get into more trouble. Turney Center was full of petty laws. There was a policy of being allowed to wear your own clothes, your own colored t-shirt, your Levi's, your own shoes, as a mark of privilege for good behavior.

We went to draw our clothes, and I was offered large leather boots. I had been a vegetarian and had used no animal products for a number of years. I explained that the shoes I had were adequate, and that I could do without the leather boots. I said, "Give them to someone else who needs them, and doesn't care if they wear them or not."

I was immediately ordered to draw leather boots.

"But I don't want leather boots, thank you. I don't care to have leather boots."

To them, it wasn't just that I didn't want to wear the state shoes. It was that if I didn't wear the state shoes, it was a mark of social position in their system.

Through a series of changes, I was sent to solitary confinement in the section of the penitentiary referred to as "the hole". I went through a browbeating session with the wardens, who told me that, because of my refusal to wear leather boots, I could begin a chain of progress where I could lose my good time, my honor time, my chance for work release and my chance for early parole.

The warden said to the assistant warden,

"Well, you know how he is. All you have to do is order him to wear the boots. He won't wear the boots, so we pop him and give him a reprimand. Then we order him to wear the boots. And you know how he is; he ain't gonna wear the boots. So then, because it's his second offense, we get to give him a couple of days in the hole. So we give him a couple of days in the hole, and we order him to wear the boots. And you *know* he ain't gonna wear the boots. Then we get to give him ten days in the hole. Then we order him to wear the boots. By this time, it's getting up to third offense, and getting pretty serious. Might have to go for thirty days in the hole. And then we order him to wear the boots. He probably ain't gonna roll over. He probably won't wear the boots. By this time, we have enough charges on him, we start getting to chip into his good time, he starts losing his good behavior time, starts losing his honor time. We can turn this one year into three years for him."

I felt like I was being compressed in a vise. And like he said, I couldn't roll over for it. But it squeezed me so hard, it squeezed tears from my eyes.

He sent me back to my cell—my room, in all fairness. We had nice individual rooms at Turney Center. There was a glass window in the door. When the guard came and peeked in your window at night to see if you were in bed, he got a noseprint on your glass. If you didn't have the noseprint polished off by the next inspection time, you got demerits.

They had a system down there that was supposed to encourage you to straighten up. It was behavior modification in its worst form. Thought up by psychologists, tested on rats and implemented by the local farmers' sons, driven by recession to seek work in the pen.

The small pressures carried into the Visiting Room, where we were written tickets like traffic tickets for touching our loved ones. I got two smooch tickets in one visiting hour once, and had to receive a warning. I saw that behavior mod was a way to break people's souls. I thought, *Isn't there some small thing I could leave here that would be of help to the people that come here later?* I felt myself like a donkey being pierced with a goad and lured by a carrot. I tried to teach the other prisoners the nature of conditioning. I told them,

"Walk fast enough to avoid the goad.
"Do not reach for the carrot."

I hope that little poem still lives at Turney Center.

My counselor called me to his office and said, "They're going to lock you up. You can have a phone call here; you still have a phone call coming since you've been transferred to a new prison."

I called my family and said,

"They got me cold. They're going to lock me up. I ain't going to be able to communicate with you. Whatever you do, you have to do from the outside, because I can't do anything any more. I'm going to go to the hole."

And I was sent to the hole. They gave me a pair of

coveralls built for someone about five-six, which fit so poorly on my six-foot four that I had to zip it up to mid-stomach and tie the arms together around my chest, with my shoulders sticking out the top, like the mad drag of a penitentiary ball gown. To get a shirt, I had to ask to see the chaplain, and I had to ask the chaplain if he would tell them to let me have a shirt.

I settled in, and I had always promised myself that I was going to read the Bible if I was ever seriously locked up. I looked at the Bible, and I didn't start reading it right away, because I figured I might have to do so much time there, why use it up too soon. And then, miraculously, that afternoon, word came that we were being transferred. We came out of our cells, blinking like coming out of caves, Brandon, my partner who had gone to the hole also, and I. They took us to the trusty camp, and they gave us our mail, which had been held back from us for days. They told us we were free to have visitors, and my family was there with a picnic lunch, and they let me go have lunch with my family. I said,

"How in the world did this happen? How did you guys pull me out of the hole into a picnic? How did this happen?"

They said, "We went to Commissioner Bass. First, we went to Sears and bought some good, heavy plastic work boots. We took them down and showed them to Mr. Bass, and said, 'Stephen will wear these work boots, and he'll do whatever work you tell him to do. He just doesn't want to wear leather boots. If you let him have these plastic boots, he won't be any trouble.' "

Commissioner Bass knew me from talking with me up in Unit Five, and he knew that I was not putting anybody on. I was trying to work within what I felt was the rights and privileges a human being has under the Constitution.

Commissioner Bass had told my family,

"No, I don't mind your coming to see me. I wish other prisoners had somebody who cared about them who would come and see me, and try to help them out. It's the ones that haven't got anybody to come see me or help them out who are the ones in trouble, the ones who really need the help."

He seemed like such a sane, kind, human man.

Well, when the Republicans pulled a *coup d'etat* just before Governor Alexander was due to be sworn in, by taking the government away from Governor Blanton, we thought things would change in Tennessee. Even the legislature saw that things might change. Governor Alexander called for a man, one Bradley who was in corrections in Washington state, to come straighten out our penitentiary. The legislature said,

"It's against the law in Tennessee for someone from out of state to be offered such a high Tennessee state job."

The legislature was asked to change that. They made the change, and Bradley was brought to Tennessee, and was questioned before the legislature. They asked him,

"Do you intend to fire Mr. Bass?"

"No," Bradley replied, "I do not intend to fire Mr. Bass."

When Bradley took over, he demoted Mr. Bass from Assistant Commissioner of Corrections, and gave him another post where his influence was limited to a very small number of men. There are thousands of men in the Tennessee state corrections system, and as Assistant Commissioner, Mr. Bass had access to most of them. In the job he was transferred to, his access was limited to a few hundred men.

There was not a conscious quota system that caused Mr. Bass to be a black Assistant Commissioner and Mr. Luttrell a white Commissioner; it was something which had evolved from the people of Tennessee, not through any kind of federal court order. It had a kind of homely justice to it. Everyone appreciated that there was a strong, intelligent, compassionate black man high up in Corrections. It made Tennessee look better that he was there. For Mr. Bradley to fire him, remove him from his position of influence, was a piece of insensitivity that he may regret when he has been in the South a little longer, and understands it a little better.

I hope nobody thinks I just like Mr. Bass because he was good to me; but I have to say that when you are a prisoner, any kindness that is shown shines like the morning sun.

CRC/NCRC

There are people in the administration of the prison and among the guards who are some of the kindest and most decent people I have met and worked in public with. Real public servants. Diamond Jim, our warden at the Walls, was a pretty decent guy; but he didn't command the emotional loyalty that Bigfoot did.

Warden Moore had once had command of Brushy Mountain, and had asked to run an honor unit for some of the prisoners he felt were worth betting on. He transferred to work at the Cockrell Bend Rehabilitation Center, the smaller of Tennessee's prison farms, the larger being at Fort Pillow. He was a large, impressive man, with a shock of wavy iron-grey wiry hair, vigorous with a deep, rumbling voice, with such a large and fatherly presence that killers, robbers, and long-time criminals could look upon him unaffectedly as some sort of fatherly and helpful image. He was a man of whom it was said,

"He must have been born and bred for generations to run a maximum security institution."

Such was the rationale that they used when they transferred him to Fort Pillow. Among those in Bigfoot's care was a large, gentle, almost childlike convict serving 156 years for some crime so serious that most people wouldn't say what it was. He depended on Bigfoot, Warden Moore.

Warden Moore was transferred to Fort Pillow. Big John, which was not the prisoner's name, could not stand to be separated from Warden Moore. He applied for transfer to Fort Pillow, and was turned down.

It's pretty easy to escape from CRC. They say about eighty guys a year do. Big John went over the fence one night, and was gone for two weeks. He probably had a few steak dinners and a few drinks. He was caught, without violence, in another state, and extradited back to Tennessee.

When they were taking him back he said,

"I wasn't really trying to escape. I know you ain't going to let a guy like me, with a hundred and fifty-six years on him, run loose. You would hunt me down and catch me. But I thought if I just went out for a couple of weeks and did something a little bit bad, that you wouldn't call me a trusty anymore, and would send me to Fort Pillow with Mr. Moore."

I was at CRC when Warden Moore returned after an extended time at Fort Pillow. He was visiting his friends at CRC, walking down through the middle of the rows of bunks arranged much like a military barracks. People gathered from all ends to come find Mr. Moore and shake his hand, and the vibes were very good. It felt a little glowy and a little tingly. It was honest-to-God love and affection and good vibes between Mr. Moore and some serious convicts.

All prison guards aren't bad. Most prison guards aren't bad. Warden Moore didn't think of himself in emotional terms; he just felt you should give a man a fair break, and was a heavy presence in the Tennessee state prison system.

After Bigfoot left CRC, I put in a transfer to leave. I had been content to spend my time on a prison farm until I got out; but when Bigfoot left, he was replaced by a psychologist type from the treatment side; and we soon found that for chicken manure, the psychologist type from the treatment side beats a maximum security warden every time.

I had the same lesson driven home even further at the work release center, NCRC in Nashville. When I first came to NCRC, I didn't like the director, Mr. T. My dislike for Mr. T. stemmed from the night he had us all ordered out of bed and dragged over to the basketball court, where he chewed our tail in a severe, loud voice for a couple of hours over the question of some people going out the back door. I didn't like being hollered at.

But as I got to know him, I began to respect what he was doing more and more. I saw that Mr. T. would holler and scream and rage, but he wouldn't send you back to the Walls unless it was just. And that being hollered and raged at was to keep from sending you back to the Walls, to not revoke your chance. I learned this when Mr. T. left and once again we got another non-correction type, an ex-chaplain from the treament side. Once again I saw that as far as chicken manure goes, pound for pound, a chaplain from the treatment side is worse than a maximum security warden. Many people were sent back to the Walls and lost their chance; impersonal signs on the walls took the place of shouting.

In the penitentiary, it is sometimes true as C. S. Lewis said, that more and more terrible things can be done in the name of treatment than the Constitution would permit in the name of punishment.

Nashville Jaycees

Several years after I returned from prison, I was in Nashville addressing the Nashville Junior Chamber of Commerce. I had a warm reception, with a lot of good friendship shown, and respect for our overseas programs. It amused me that for some of my action I get to go on the rubber chicken circuit. I left the meeting feeling friendly and well-handled by the young Nashville businessmen I had met.

In the parking lot, the young black attendant had a friend hanging out with him in the little booth in the middle of the parking lot. It was about a block-square parking lot, with a little kiosk in the middle. As I came up to pay the parking fee, the attendant looked at me and said,

"Don't I know you?"

I said, "Me?"

He said, "Weren't you in the slam?"

I said, "Yeah, I was up in the walls."

He said to his friend, "I know this dude here. He's all right."

His friend looked at him somewhat askance, for opening up on an intimate level with a white person, as if it might not be quite safe. The attendant saw his friend's unease, and in a perfectly spontaneous gesture, one which seems to me quite subtle, although very difficult to communicate to "straight" folks (straight in the convict's sense of one who has not been in prison), he said,

"Hey, man. This is my nigger. This is my nigger, man."

His friend immediately looked closely at my face to see if there was anything in me that could not stand to be called "my nigger".

I didn't mind. We talk rough in the joint, and I saw it for the friendly gesture that it was, and responded in kind.

If freedom was like light, that parking lot would have glowed.

I've told friends, mostly white people, that story, and they almost never understand.

As I came home, I counted my blessings that I could be friends with those young businessmen in the Chamber of Commerce, and still be straight with my prison friends.

Chapter XXVII

This is the chapter where my friends told me that it wouldn't really be cool or smart to list all of the policemen who have told me they smoked marijuana while they were either investigating me or arresting me for smoking marijuana, and all of the counselors and psychologists who told me they smoked marijuana while they were candling my head to see if I was crazy because I smoked marijuana.

The Crimeless Victims

The system as it now stands, is doomed, by reason of obsolescence. The values that are predicated by that system are counter to the priorities of humankind, animalkind, and the rest of kind.

The system was never valid; but when it was viable, it worked on unlimited resources. Now it works not on unlimited resources, but intensive care. The supposed free enterprise system has a tube in every vein and orifice, dripping stimulants and depressants, antibiotics, defoliants, into a decaying carcass.

I am as much a believer that this is the end of civilization-as-we-know-it as any Armageddon addict. I am optimistic and prayerful that it can be accomplished without a general world collapse, economically, militarily, culturally, before the new system has evolved itself sufficiently to carry the weight of all our friends and relations.

Fuller, Toffler, Rifkin, all of the freelance non-governmental analysts, all agree that patchwork and repair will not suffice; only redesign will save our village.

The entire restrictive/contractive viewpoint of corrections and social problems is counterproductive. The tendency of society is to come down more and more harshly on the criminal; and the tendency of the criminal is to forget the crime he committed to become incarcerated in the light of the oppression which continues against him. He considers himself less and less a criminal, and more and more a revolutionary. In fact, the same incident can be considered crime or revolution.

Somehow, our society understands that better when we're talking about Jesse James, Quantrell's Raiders or the Dalton Boys, than they do in the 1980's.

In the same way, to an American, Pancho Villa is an outlaw; to a Mexican he is one of the fathers of the country.

The equivalent of that today is obviously the I.R.A. The I.R.A. is not primarily involved in robbery, but in death and destruction, which seems to be a greater indicator of political intent. Although they have more of a political organization than a crime organization, their tactics have placed them, in the eyes of Margaret Thatcher, irretrievably in the ranks of criminals, in spite of their political intent.

The unclear boundary line over which Margaret Thatcher and the I.R.A. disagree can almost be described as the line that is crossed in von Clausewitz' *Vom Krieg*, where he says that war is merely the logical extension of politics.

They are not fighting over Bobby Sands; they are fighting over William of Orange. This is a family feud among the people that has been carried on for almost eight hundred years. It is one of the clearest examples on earth that an oppressed people do not submit; although you may kill individuals, the truth lives on in the minds of the people and cannot be destroyed until there is a conscious effort of love and forgiveness on both sides. To forgive each other for what we have cumulatively done to each other over several hundred years, and to recognize the unity of the island is the only balm that can heal the wounds that have been inflicted.

In order to understand the depths of the feelings in the I.R.A., Americans need to understand a little of the history of Ireland. All the Americans know about the Potato Famine, when all the Irish came to the United States. The Irish starved by thousands. But what the Americans do not know is that during the same time as the Potato Famine, there was meat and milk and bread in Ireland, which was being exported to England as export crops, for the sake of the absentee landlords.

170

The situation is identical in Central America today.

These are the issues that are carried down from father to son. There is no forgetting until the reminders of the injustice, which are unfair political divisions of the people, are removed.

Although some Irish and some Indians are driven to violence by their frustrations, we cannot be blinded by that violence to the truth of their cause.

We speak of the victimless crime, such as marijuana smoking, which is defined by the state as a crime although there is no victim. In the case of the Indians, the Irish, the Salvadoreans, it is not a case of the victimless crime, but of the crimeless victim. There are many victims, but no one has defined a crime. The American Indians say,

"A crime has clearly been committed."

The government says,

"We didn't do it. We weren't alive when that happened."

And the Indians say,

"Neither were we. But we live by it. It affects our life. It informs our entire way of being and our culture."

It relates to Bucky's teaching on the true definition of indemnity through incorporation. When a company takes a venture, it is insured against loss; but the workers are not indemnified. "Incorporated" and "Limited" are old legal precedents by royal decree, that the losses of the company shall be limited. But the sailors who are lost at sea, leaving families behind, are not indemnified.

In the same way that a royal decree by custom passes down to us as a law and a way of organization for the legal system, the technical definition of non-criminality for the actions of our forefathers is passed down to us who are the clear beneficiaries of the crime, *i.e.,* the holders of the swag. Old cultures, global cultures move very slowly. Of necessity, they recognized the maintaining of the generations in their politics, and expected continuity for their people. If you made a treaty with a people, that treaty was made with those people and would continue in effect, unlike the United States where, if you make a treaty under one administration, it is repudiated in four years by the next administration, causing schizophrenia and fickleness of heart that any of us would find intolerable if dealing with a single entity.

The blacks and the Indians merely ask that the realities of four hundred years ago, three hundred years ago, two hundred years ago, be washed clean in the good will and justice of the present, rather than perpetuate the bitterness. This is the corollary of the Indians' clear, religious folk belief that the decisions of a people should reflect the results on their offspring for the next seven generations.

Chimaltenango, 1981

They say Wovoca,
who had the visions
about the dance of the Ghost Shirt,
was not understood by the Indians
who went forth in their ghost shirts,
expecting them to stop
the bullets of the cavalry.
It may be so.
There are villages in Guatemala
where the people have given up
their native dress entirely,
and turn out on Sunday mornings
in blue suits and neckties, white shirts.
I wonder if the Indians in Guatemala
who have been so touched by the *evangelicos*
will find that a rusty old black funeral suit
will stop the bullets any better
than the native *traje* will.

Guatemala

It's almost as if the multinational corporations of the world have declared war on peasants because peasants aren't cost-effective. In Guatemala, there are seven million people in the country. Four million of them live in the hills and scratch a living out of the sides of volcanoes. A million of them live in Guatemala City and run Western Civilization there. Down in Guatemala City there are billboards, Calvin Klein jeans, everything. There are a lot of poor people, but there are some rich ones.

It takes that six million, poor as they are out on the edge, to support that one million in the city. Before Western Civilization came to Guatemala, I don't know if they were Democrats or Republicans, or if they were just; but they were their own thing, and whatever they did was what they were doing to themselves. But this is something that is being done to them by, essentially, us.

There is a certain progression of civilization that was recognized by an Englishman who said, "We are all Greeks." There is much Greek thought coming up through Roman thought, into the Roman Empire, into the Holy Roman Empire—which was French—and Charlemagne, which passed into the British Empire.

The empire passed on to the United States, which is that empire now. This is the story of Western Civilization marching across the world. And it is marching right smack on South America, North America, and the Third World.

Native people all over the world are being suppressed for the sake of our style of civilization; and our style of civilization is much more expensive than theirs, and much harder on the world than theirs. The multinationals are deliberately trying to supplant their civilization with ours. They do it on purpose. They don't say they are trying to wreck the Indian civilization; they say they are trying to be cost-effective. They are trying to make a buck.

The word the Spanish used was the "reduction" of Latin America, in the Latin sense of duct, to take them off one channel and put them on another channel, the re-duction of South America. It was a program against those people's native religion that was carried out as faithfully and with as much power as the programs against those people's native lifestyles are being carried out now by the multinational corporations who are the international, multinational arm of the eighties the way that Catholicism and monarchy were four hundred years ago.

The multinationals are international economic terrorists. The people fear economically, even unto their lives. Not their savings or what they are going to do in their old age, but to their lives.

I have several friends who understand the situation in Guatemala perfectly well. One of them is a well-known, respected writer in the United States who happens to sit on the board of a clinic for the Indians in Guatemala. He said to the fellows at the clinic,

"Shall I tell your story in the United States and explain how the clinic is unable to run because of the strength of the oppression here?"

They said, "Oh! They'd just come and kill us if you did."

In the same way, I could name a lot of names in Guatemala. But right now it seems important to not cause reprisals to fall on innocent people.

Most of the aid groups in Guatemala received personal letters from the death squad, telling them to get out of the country.

Our government's stance in central America, in Guatemala,

176

El Salvador, Nicaragua, will bring shame on our nation for years to come.

Basically, the Europeans own the land. An amazing number of South American presidents have Scandinavian or German or French names. We think of South America as having been mostly done by the Spanish. But it's just Europeans. Guatemala is a European colony surrounded by an old Mayan country. The people who live there in the colony want to maintain old European standards and lifestyle. The advertisements in Guatemala are not based on the United States. When it shows a picture of a nice man's dress shirt, it says, "European quality." It doesn't say, "American quality." They don't advertise much American at all. They don't talk much about America. They don't pay much attention to America. Their eyes are cast toward Europe for culture.

PLENTY, the Farm's relief organization, went to Guatemala in 1976, immediately after the earthquake in February, and saw not only the earthquake damage, but the obvious signs of poverty and starvation on every level, which caused us immediately to try to start a project in Guatemala.

First we took carpenters, and we rebuilt after the earthquake. Then we took medical personnel, and tried to open and help with clinics. We didn't receive a lot of cooperation from the government for our medical operations, but we found that we could do diet and nutrition with their blessing. Our path was always to stay clear and not cause trouble that could draw down fire on the local residents, who live completely at the mercy of the government.

By completely at the mercy of the government, I mean that, as Amnesty International has estimated, twenty thousand covert government assassinations have been carried out in the past ten years in Guatemala.

Our project prospered in Guatemala, and we learned not only Spanish, but Indian dialects: Cakchiquel, Quiche. Our work and friendship with the Guatemalan people seemed to be completely open-ended. It looked as if we could stay there and initiate projects and raise money in the United States and really get to be a help for a lot of people who came to be our close friends. But as the situation in Nicaragua turned over, as the situation in El Salvador smoldered into a civil war, the character of Guatemala became not so much changed as that the velvet lining on the iron glove began to wear through.

University professors were killed.

Students were killed.

Civilian political candidates were killed, sometimes shot down in the street, sometimes hunted down by motorized death squads driving cars with government plates carrying men in civilian clothes with military weapons.

Then the focus shifted from the city to the country. Whole villages were massacred. People were killed in Panzos. Comalapa. San Juan Sacatepequez. Body dumps were discovered. Indians disappeared. They systematically shot the people who were working on literacy programs, radio communications programs, people's medical programs, agricultural extension help programs, because those people were organizers, and the organizers must be removed right off the top. PLENTY was forced to pull its volunteers home. Sadly, we embraced those friends we left behind, and brought as many as we could with us. We returned to the United States.

We hated to leave. We didn't leave from fear. We left because our presence was a temptation that could bring down fire on the Indians.

We lived with these people long enough for the initial politeness to have worn off. We have been together long enough for us to forget to stay on our good behavior. We have been through hassles together. We have been a hassle to one another and forgiven one another, and we have become friends. It is refreshing to bring them to the Farm, for they are some of the few who are not shocked at our lifestyle, and who understand how and why we could do such a thing.

We continue to study Spanish, Cakchiquel, and we study Sesotho from Lesotho in South Africa; and we study Gaelic, Welsh and Irish.

Americans are very bad about learning languages. They

hardly know any other languages. The rest of the world looks at them a little contemptuously because of that. A lot of people's culture is in their language. All the different languages and the different cultures of the world are very important, and we need to begin taking steps to preserve them. I heard that already in Guatemala, within the troubles of the last ten years, a couple of kinds of *traje*, or native clothes, have gone extinct, because of the violence there. We have to do something about that. We can't lose that. It is too precious.

I probably know more about the ancient Maya religion than many of the Indians do, because they have not had the advantage of reading Dr. Sylvanus Griswold Morley, who unearthed the ancient Maya and had all that stuff down pretty cold. The modern Cakchiquel have just little bits of things left over like proverbs or sayings; but they are very well Catholicized. Catholicism has been stuck on them very heavily for the past four hundred years.

Although they consider themselves Indians in culture, they don't consider themselves Indians in religion. They consider themselves Catholics, pretty deeply. But, nonetheless, Esteban Chuj has a little pyramid in his cornfield; and when he took us up to see the little pyramid in his cornfield, we observed that there was a little fire, and someone had burned a few grains of corn just recently on top of the pyramid in his cornfield.

Anybody who understands the old religion these days is pretty much considered a brujo, a witch, a wizard. Ordinary people don't really know much about the old religion.

It's interesting that their religion is something that has been pretty effectively taken away from them, although they still speak Cakchiquel and they weave their clothes and they do their Indian culture thing, more closely to their roots than most North American Indians, who do not live viably in their original lifestyle, although they may remember more of their religions.

The big countries of the world are perceived by the small countries of the world as being the dictators of the entire world. They determine the lifestyle, they determine who gets what. They—especially the United States and Russia—are so paranoid of each other that they enforce stringent measures on the world in order to counteract each other's influence; their actions are so strong as to be heavier than the entire defensive capability of the remainder of the world. Haig talks about the military options that we may use against the Soviets. But what about the military options that El Salvador may use against the United States? Now that is not parity. We are not talking forty-nine/fifty-one, or fifty-five/forty-five when we are talking about El Salvador and the United States. They are at our complete mercy, militarily.

I have heard high government officials recently speak of "our sovereign republics." How can one say "our sovereign republics"? The words "our" and "sovereign" belong in different sentences; someone else's sovereign republic cannot be our republic or it is no longer sovereign.

Reagan talks about Russia scheming on our sovereign republics; and Haig talks about "sending those Vietnamese over here to deprive these people of their civil rights." It was such a pious piece of poppycock that Haig himself almost choked saying it.

The amount of corn and beans in the diet of the peasants of Guatemala has declined since 1976, because of their treatment at the hands of the rulers of their own country and the vagaries of the world market. Guatemala is not in as desperate straits as El Salvador yet because business is still fairly good. They say Nicaragua went because Somoza didn't give the other businessmen a break. But business was fairly good in Guatemala, and there was not going to be a serious revolution until the businessmen started involving themselves with it. In Guatemala, the million people who live in Guatemala City—many of whom are poor, but a number of whom are quite rich—control the remaining six million people of the entire country, more than sixty per cent of whom are Indians who would rather be living a different lifestyle, who do not want a "western" lifestyle, and would prefer to remain the way they were. These people are being dragged into a tax-producing, central-government-supporting, "modern" economy unwillingly. They went from a self-induced, if primitive level, to an even more primitive level, where they are not allowed to care for themselves, or farm or gather food where they will; or cut firewood where they will, where they must figure out how to get money out of an economy which doesn't have any money, in order to support high rise hotels and the rows and rows of Caterpillar heavy equipment dealers, all the European, Japanese, Chinese equipment dealers in the city. The peasants are forced to carry the weight of developing Guatemala into an industrialized country when it isn't even good for Guatemala to be an industrialized country. The establishment has no compassion for the lifestyle of the people in the country. The Indians in Solola raise potatoes and onions which they don't even like to eat, but which they can sell.

"What can you grow here? We don't want your corn. Who in the city eats corn, peasant? We ain't living on corn and beans."

Potatoes and onions now grow on the ground which used to provide the corn and beans the people ate. All the best of everything must be sold, with the remainders and the culls being kept for the people. The people don't like that, and rebel against it. For their rebellion, the government sends forth troops and kills them, shoots them, tortures them, dumps their bodies over cliffs, to defend the contention of fifteen percent of the country that wants to live like the United States wants to live. It is appalling.

We have known for years about the conditions taking place in Guatemala. We heard stuff from our Indian friends about the massacre at Panzos and the body dump at Comalapa months before the stories broke in the states. We even know about the jet air strike north of Solola that has not yet been spoken of in the states.

When we first heard these stories, we waited for verification, because we heard them purely by word of mouth from Indian friends, sometimes across more than one language. But as time went on, our whisper line among the Indian people in Guatemala was very accurate, and the things they told us proved up and came out into the open again and again.

It is significant that the hippies can know something for years and years and be unable to make a difference in our native country because there are so many lies and everything is discounted as propaganda. This is the essence of the Big Lie technique. We here in the United States, even now, suffer under the media manipulations that were called, when used by Hitler, the technique of the Big Lie.

It is very difficult to know what is really going on. It requires effort on your part, or you aren't going to get to know what's happening.

In World War II, we went in and whipped the Germans and accused them of war crimes for what they did to their people, among others. In El Salvador, we are on the other side.

The people of Guatemala are being held hostage. The gang that runs the government in Guatemala is no more lawful than the gang that took the hostages in Iran.

Haig talks about outsiders coming in and depriving the Central Americans of their civil rights. What civil rights has anyone in Guatemala had since 1954 when the CIA engineered a coup of their government and stuck in a bunch of puppet generals who have been running it by election fraud and terrorism ever since? What civil rights does anyone in Guatemala have who isn't a general? There aren't any civil rights in Guatemala for civilians. The last civilian candidate for President was shot down in the streets of Guatemala City by a large squad of militarily-equipped assassins.

They pick them all off. Government troops went down and shot all the university professors who had liberal ideas. They shot all the university students who were brave and led demonstrations.

During the Carter administration, there was much criticism of President Carter for his commitment to human rights. Much of the criticism stemmed from the idea that we were rocking the boat and stirring up trouble. In particular, people meant that Russia considered Carter's statements as accusations; and many people felt the President should pursue a course that didn't advertise that so much, to avoid making people mad when we didn't have to.

At the same time, another criticism of his stance on human rights was that it was basically impotent, a piece of mouth that hotted things up, but that was not reflected in the actual policy, and didn't actually make any difference to anyone, but was just a statement. As his human rights stance became unpopular, he tried to become more specific in his statements. Among other things, he pinpointed Guatemala and four other nations in South America as being the worst offenders in that part of the world.

Guatemala was identified as one of the five worst military dictatorships in Latin America during the time we were there. We could see the results when the President of Guatemala turned certain aid back to the United States, and refused to allow certain U.S. aid into the country as a protest against Carter's statements on human rights.

Also, the right-wing death squad killings continued to take place in Guatemala, Honduras, El Salvador. Critics of Carter's human rights stance pointed to the continuation of this repression and killings as more proof that his position was basically an impotent one.

Under those circumstances, it was hard to counter those allegations. But subsequent events have shown trends that tend to support President Carter. The first that came to our attention was the open word in Central America, and especially in Guatemala and El Salvador, that if Reagan won the election, he would de-emphasize Carter's human rights program, although his main criticisms had been that it was ineffective, rather than that it was too effective. When Reagan's people in Central America said that Reagan was going to support the military rulers because they were technically or officially "anti-Communist", the answer to Carter's critics became apparent.

Unbelievably, things got worse. There *had* been some effect in the United States' criticism of inhumane acts; and

183

as soon as the United States withdrew its criticism, those inhumane acts multiplied. The military rulers of Central America thought they had a clear mandate from the United States to use military and deadly force to suppress what they refer to as the "communist uprising".

The results of Reagan and Haig's foreign policy became immediately apparent in Central America. Even excluding the military aid to the El Salvadoran government, it was quite obvious that the military regimes of Central America were materially aided by Reagan's and Haig's statements that human rights would be de-emphasized in this administration, and that human rights would not be a high priority.

This is easy to see on an international level, which is why there is so much dust being thrown in the air, insisting that the rebels in Central America are Soviet- and Cuban-backed revolutionary forces that, as Haig said, are engineered from Russia to deprive Central Americans of their civil rights. Either Haig is not aware of decades of severe political repression in Central America, in which case he does not know enough to be Secretary of State; or he knows it and is hiding it or ignoring it, in which case he is too dishonest to be Secretary of State.

It is plain to any visitor who has spent any time in Central America that for all these decades, the economic and social climate that the United States has allowed and even fostered, a short few hundred miles distant from its border— the military regimes which have been installed with the help of the United States Marines and the CIA, the interfering in Central American governments' internal affairs and the toppling of governments—is the root cause of the oppression that creates a revolutionary atmosphere in Central America.

If someone came in to your average rich American suburban neighborhood with a truckload of guns and said,

"You can have these guns if you'll just go start rebelling against the government," the people who live in those suburban houses would call the FBI, the CIA, the state police, the local police, the sheriff, everybody in sight, and say,

"There's maniac gun peddlers here. Come get these guns out of our neighborhood!"

Our country is not severely enough oppressed to cause the people to resort to revolution. If the people of El Salvador are so oppressed that the mere presence of a weapon causes them to revolt against the government, one may not reasonably conclude that the gun was the cause of the revolution. One must look to the root causes, which are basically found in America's cupidity toward the natural resources of Central America, and North America's cynical ignoring of the condition of the peasants and the Indians of Central America.

CODA:
Tecun Uman & Pedro de Alvarado

Tecun Uman was the king of a large, fertile valley in Guatemala whose territory was invaded by the *conquistadores*, headed by Pedro de Alvarado.

The battle was not long in doubt. The Mayans tried to fight, but the Spanish had horses and guns and steel. At some point, Tecun Uman decided there was only one thing he could do with honor, and he abandoned his throne and command post and went to the front line and demanded to meet Pedro de Alvarado, the Spanish commander, in single combat.

Tecun Uman met Pedro de Alvarado in single combat, and lost.

I tried to tell this story once, to a very New Age lady at a New Age party. When I tried to tell what happened to Tecun Uman, my voice broke and my throat filled up and I could not speak. I stood on the edge of a sob, and the lady looked at me and said,

"Please finish. I'll go the trip with you if you'll just tell me so I can understand."

And I couldn't even.

It was not just the story of Pedro de Alvarado and Tecun Uman, but that an old man I know carries a piece of the history of Guatemala in a verbal fashion, passed down in the oral tradition. It is not something from a history book. What Juan knows has been passed down from storyteller to storyteller, similar to the *griots* in *Roots*, the story of Tecun Uman going out to meet Pedro de Alvarado.

This is to say that in the simplest and clearest fashion possible, the people have not forgotten the conquest. The people remember the conquest. I know an old man who is one of the people who remembers.

And the people remember the partition of Ireland.

And the partition of Pakistan.

And the partition of Palestine.

And the American Indians remember Wounded Knee.

And the black Americans remember that they do have roots in Africa, and they did not come here by choice.

Politicians wish to move great masses of people. We do not need to move great masses of anyone. We need to let the bitterness of the moves we have already accomplished die down.

The Empire

Near the end of 1980, I traveled to New Zealand in the company of several friends, including Chief Oren Lyons of the Onondaga nation. One of the people we met in New Zealand who was of particular interest was Dun Mehaka, a true natural chief of the Maori people, although not a chief in the formal sense. Seventeen and a half stone, that's two hundred forty-three pounds in American, about six feet even. No fat. Wearing green military fatigue hat with giant Chinese red star and a pair of red swimming pants, he was of immense stature. Tim Shadbolt's friend, Dun Mehaka.

Dun told Oren and me why he had become a Marxist.

He held up his hand and clenched his fist. The flat, square face of his fist was covered with small semicircles of white scars.

He said,

"See all those marks? Those are people's teeth. I fought against them as hard as I could. I fought like ten niggers, and I couldn't win. So I became a Marxist."

And that is the thing that Bruce, the kiwi in the street, needs to look at and understand. When a man is naturally intelligent, and a natural warrior, and has unlimited strength and courage, and there is no way in their system he could win, it is their fault he became a Marxist, and they created him.

Part of the Maori culture, and part of a strong warrior tradition, Dun Mehaka is a pure type of the warrior fighting chief. In him could be seen the danger of tribal and natural peoples turning from their real and self-derived natural ways for any western discipline, capitalist or socialist.

The agreement in New Zealand was not ratified by the rest of the Maori tribe. A lot of people say it isn't a real treaty.

The way the British Empire was run had you about ninety percent by the legal short hairs; and the other ten percent you were supposed to be too polite to complain about. This is the way they really conquered the world.

In New Zealand, we were talking to this man named Bruce. He had white hair, was a healthy, good looking Englishman in shorts, standing by this car he was working on. He was funny in several ways. He said that what it was about was fear, and that eventually somebody has to establish fear. Oren and I went two or three changes with him, suggesting respect and other gentler things. He held out that it was fear, that somebody had to put fear on somebody and that was how it worked.

He also said he would be willing to go out and drop a hand grenade down the exhaust pipe of one of the bulldozers working for the gold mining companies. He said,

"It'd only slow them down for a couple of days, but maybe somebody would do it again in a couple of days."

He was one of the guys in New Zealand who was suspicious of Tim Shadbolt, who is as honest a revolutionary as I have met.

Tim Shadbolt ain't polite. He won't quit complaining. Bruce felt that New Zealand had demonstrated against the war, and gotten out of the war. Then Tim took on another cause. And another cause. They accuse him of blowing with the wind. He doesn't. He just takes what's next on his list, or whomever he feels needs the help.

They tried to start a commune. They wrote it into the bylaws of the land agreement that it took all of them to agree to do anything with it. The land now sits idle because they can't agree on anything to do with it. Tim suggested turning fifty-one percent ownership over to the Maoris and inviting a bunch of Maoris to join in; and one person there doesn't want

188

to do it, so they're stymied. The one person who doesn't want
to do it says Tim just wants to let them come because of his
guilt. Tim's family is one of the families that did it to New
Zealand, and he knows that.

Consensus minus one.

The young people say that Tim is just painfully honest;
and Bruce says he blows with the wind. Ina May told her
friend Eric about him. Eric is a gentle dude, an old man,
sixty-five or seventy, white beard, tan, Saint John's
Ambulance Service uniform, doesn't trust Tim Shadbolt;
says he's just a shit disturber. There is something about Tim
that deeply troubles honest New Zealanders of even some
revolutionary heart—Bruce was willing to drop a hand
grenade down a bulldozer's exhaust pipe—it's that sense of
English politeness which Tim violates so badly that they
can't hack it. He reminded me of Richard Pryor. Fiercely
dedicated intensity.

The American mining companies are buying huge gold
mining options in New Zealand. Nobody in New Zealand
wants to do it but the government. The government wants to
do it because New Zealand doesn't have a good balance of
payments. But the country is wealthy. Everybody is well-fed.
There is virtually no poverty; even poor people look fat.
There are three million people and ninety million sheep, and
who knows how many million cows. There is a lot of meat in
the markets, and a lot of cheese.

The government goes along with it for the balance of
payments, but it isn't needed for the good of the people. It's
needed for the book-balancing at the governmental level.

New Zealand has contributed tremendously to the wealth
of the world. The gold rush that came through San Francisco
and wiped out miles of land between the mountains and
Sacramento had come from Waihi in New Zealand, and hit
the San Francisco area on its way to Alaska. It was the same
gold rush, and the reason they raised such hell in California
was that they got good at it, having practiced up in New
Zealand first. They raised hell with New Zealand and their
scars are still standing; and they're back, with more sophisti-

cated equipment that will get more gold out of poorer ore. They're talking about dumping the dross out at sea, uncaring that the sea bottom is an ecology. Amex. Amoco.

New Zealand was in World War II; the Anzacs were the combined Australian/New Zealand armies. They lost more men per capita than any country in the war, according to one guy I talked to over there. They really lost a lot. Japan was right on their closest edge. Borneo was one of the next islands over. They may have had Japanese on the continent. I'm not sure. They at least got seriously bombed. There's a pretty strong pacifist sentiment down there. A lot of folks dig country music too. That's one of the things they took from the United States, country music and a lot of the attitudes that go along with it. Country music is heavy message music.

Although it may not be common, it is heard of that the Maoris are referred to as niggers. The English have a habit of going everywhere in the world and referring to people in their own country as niggers. It's one of the Englishmen's trips. It's like Eileen Caddy said, the reason the sun doesn't set on the British Empire is because God doesn't trust the British after dark.

I used to go to Canada or Australia and start talking about the local action, and people would say,

"You're an American. How can you come in here and start talking about the action?"

But when I went to New Zealand with Chief Oren Lyons, he said,

"Here's where it's really at. The English made the same deal everywhere they went."

A big piece of this expansion out in the world right now belongs to them. We have to deal with that.

The English weren't good about learning other languages. Everywhere they went, they tended to put their own language and their own culture down on it.

When we went to Australia a few years ago, we arrived after a funny thing had happened. The Australians had elected their first social government ever. That government had done things like hire women and hire aborigines, and create a government board to deal with the aborigines. That was in 1973 to 1975. Australia had not had an official government board to deal with the aborigines until 1973. This Government was the Gough Whitlam government.

They were doing those changes, and it scared the right wingers in Australia. At the same time, there was a man who was the Queen's Governor-General. They didn't pay much attention to him; they would drag him out for parades, where he would put on his plume and do the parades, but they didn't think he was very heavy. But the Gough Whitlam government strayed too far from the path, and the Governor-General fired the government.

The Australian people were amazed. They said,

"We thought we had a Constitution! What happened to the Constitution? The Queen's Governor-General just fired the government. What's happening?"

In this century, we do not adequately understand what it means that Prince Charles is the Prince of Wales. But the people who live in Wales understand. They understand it as a symbol that when England took Wales, they owned it to such an extent that the King of England could give Wales to his son. They understand. But that symbolism is lost on our generation because it is something that happened a long time ago.

In order that the lesson not be lost on our generation, they tried to make Prince Charles Governor-General of Australia.

We hippies are very similar to the Royal Family. We, like them, vote every day, not just on election day. We vote with our lifestyle; so do they.

Prince Charles is supposed to, as is the long-agreed-upon tradition in England, maintain a neutrality in the Royal Family and allow the government to take care of the politics, and just be the Prince of Wales and go about his business.

Lady Diana has sufficiently noble lineage that she can become Queen of England. That's more of them voting with their lifestyle. Prince Charles does not have to make political statements about how he'd like the auto industry run, or how he'd like the labor unions to behave, or what he wants the government to do about foreign policy: by being the King, he espouses the most reactionary viewpoint possible. He is as far right as he can be while remaining relatively decent, which he is only relatively. He is some of the ruling oligarchy of the planet, and his mother is one of the fourteen richest women in the world—and he's not doing badly, either. It is unnecessary for him to make political statements. Those people who are of his party run the country the way he wants it run.

The authority that chartered out a great deal of the exploitation of the world is still in existence, the succession of the British Throne and all of the companies it chartered out: the East India Company, the Hudson's Bay Company, the New Zealand Company, the Rhodes Company in Africa, the West India Company. Technically, one ought to be able to sue that authority for the excesses committed by those companies, whether or not any of the corporate directors who did it then are still alive. Of course there are carefully inserted statutes of limitations that keep the companies protected.

The Queen is a source of free will. It's very simple, because what it comes down to is, *nobody tells her what to do.* And when you're getting told what to do by her, you're getting told by the least number of people.

The theory is that if she's good and just, the people will keep her in action.

Since she is the benchmark for free will, she in combination with the church fulfill the sacraments, which is why it's religious at all. *Regina per gratia dei.*

All social position is measured against her. Everybody who subscribes to the social position of the Queen—even the Labour Party, supporting the sovereignty of the British Isles—supports the Queen. The Queen is not a figurehead.

The revolution of 1776 was basically a collectivist revolution which held that the people, collectively, held the sovereignty that had been held by the royalty for the people up until then. It was a collectivization of sovereignty. And it lasted quite a while. Maybe until the era of the robber barons, who were instrumental in changing America's orientation away from collectivity into pursuit of individual wealth.

The Queen is referred to as "our sovereign lady." She holds the sovereignty. She is a symbol of the sovereignty of the country. Like the royal family, we hippies are a symbol for the sovereignty of our people, too. People notice that we have achieved some measure of sovereignty and say, "Well, it's easy for you guys; you guys have sovereignty."

What is real about sovereignty for our people is that no one gave it to us. We expressed it, like extruding it. We produced it, invented it, created it and maintain it. We declared sovereignty by declaring free will. From that, we saw that individuals have the power to make agreements, and to consolidate themselves into groups. Our culture derives its sovereignty from the individual sovereignty of its citizens, rather than deriving its sovereignty from a hereditary sovereign. This is government by consent of the governed. Everything we do is a declaration of our sovereignty.

Our sovereignty is not our freedom; our sovereignty is what guarantees our freedom. Some people think that whatever measure of freedom they have is just the environment, like air. Tim Shadbolt points out that every freedom we have, somebody fought for; and if we don't keep fighting for them, we will diminish the freedoms we pass on, rather than augment them.

By living in collectivity with a minimum of governmental structures, we demonstrate that our basic nature is sufficiently good that we do not have to be forced or bullied into living correctly. I am not kept from stealing by the laws of the state.

To understand sovereignty is to understand the sovereignty of other people, to recognize that my sovereignty diminishes no one else's. Everyone has to have sovereignty, or they cannot live free.

What the Indians are trying to tell the United States is,
We have a source of sovereignty. We do not want to hook

*on to the secondhand source of the United States. We have a
source.*

This has so far been unrecognized by the government of
the United States which says,

*No one inside the borders of the United States has
sovereignty but the United States of America. These reservations are merely land that we allotted you to live on, out of
the goodness of our hearts.*

And the Indians say,

*Nonsense. This is our land. This was always our land. We
reserved these small parts for us to live on. It is part of our
original land, which we never gave you. It belongs to us from
the beginning of history.*

The center of the ongoing skirmishes between the Indians
and the United States is based in the idea that the United
States refuses to allow sovereignty to the original people of
the continent. But those Indians who retain their native
languages and keep faith with their native beliefs and
continue to remember their ways, and to honor their elders,
and to live as if every motion they made mattered unto the
seventh generation, express their sovereignty anyway, and,
like them, everything we do expresses not just our freedom,
but our sovereignty, which is our right to our freedom.

As Long as the Grass Shall Grow

The American Indians have a legitimate argument against the United States because they have been treated in a racist fashion, casually and arrogantly.

I was raised in the Southwest. I went to school with Indians, and have known Indian people all my life. I am comfortable around Indian people. As a citizen of the United States, it is appalling to me that my country could allow so much injustice to happen. These people have been oppressed continually, from the very first moment we came to this country, right up until now, just like they say.

If the FBI doesn't like me to say that, or if the Republicans don't like it, it's tough. As long as this country and others sweep that kind of oppression under the rug, it is very difficult for us to try to talk justice to any other countries in the world. We answer just claims in an adversary fashion that makes it so that even when the Indians win, only the lawyers prosper. We are not dealing justice in our own country.

One of the things the United States has lost from being a polyglot culture is some of the integrity that an individual culture can have. It is at least tacitly understood that it is worthless to make a treaty if the first generation of people that you made the treaty with are not going to pass that treaty down to their children.

Just because our ancestors are all dead who robbed the Indians of their land and kidnapped and enslaved the

Africans, doesn't mean we don't have a debt. The descendants of those Africans and those Indians who are, even now, sundered from their land, are still trying for the sovereignty by law that was once theirs by right. They are still suffering the results of those acts for which the rest of the country refuses to shoulder the responsibility. The United States is not homogenous enough to be a coherent people.

When the Hau De No Sau Nee, (pronounced Ho-De-No-Sho-Nee, called "Iroquois" by the French) or the Dine (DEE-NAY, called "Navajo" by the Spanish) or the Arapaho made a treaty, it was meant that the tribe would always honor that treaty. It was a matter of the honor of the Hau De No Sau Nee people, or the honor of the Dine people, or the honor of the Lakota people, that they would honor their end of these agreements. To an intact culture, our polyglot culture looks like a culture with no honor that doesn't care whether the agreements that were made in its name are kept or not.

One of the ways they got the Indians to give up their land was to divide up their land into allotments of 160 acres. Then the Indians who owned the allotments could sell the allotments and the white men could buy them out like a checkerboard.

When Congress talks about the termination of the Indian program, they mean that the Indians are totally folded into a middle-class life in the United States and no longer exist as an ethnic entity. The Indians consider that genocide. And it *is* genocide. But the government officials have no recognition of that.

The government officials also are anxious to sterilize Indian women, so they won't have babies and go on welfare. And there aren't many Indians left. The Indians consider that if you take a bunch of people and put them on a small piece of ground that isn't very good, and then they're starving on that piece of ground, that before you come in and sterilize them, you could see about improving the ground or giving them some more ground to live on. Sterilization and relocation is clearly a policy of termination of the Indians.

Termination is the official policy of the Mexican government: that all the Mexican Indians should be turned into being Mexicans, citizens of Mexico. It is not that we did this two hundred years ago; but we are doing this in the United States now; we are doing it in Mexico now; we are doing it in Guatemala now, and in every North, Central and South American country from Canada to Argentina. We are still "reducing" the Indians as the Spanish said.

Twenty-five tribes in the interior of Brazil are threatened by a genocidal plan equivalent to germ warfare, to be financed by loans to the Brazilian government from the World Bank, whose money largely comes from the taxpayers of the United States. These are tribes who have had almost no previous contact with "civilization", and who have therefore almost no immunities or antibodies to "civilized" diseases such as the common cold and measles. The Brazilian government plans to develop the jungles of the Amazon, to turn it into farmland and to mine its unbelievably rich deposits of minerals and ores. Of what consequence is the existence of twenty-five small tribes in the interior of Brazil when weighed in the balance with all those fabled riches? Of what consequence was the Red Man in North America two hundred years ago? Or today?

It does not destroy an Indian's culture to give him a radio so he can speak his own language over it. It does not destroy a Third World people's culture to learn some new things that make the living of life easier. We have learned many things as a planetary culture which have not yet been transmitted to the Third World. To oppress them by removing value from their culture and their language and their ways so that they must abandon them for the culture and the language and the ways of the oppressors—of the conquerors—although you don't kill their physical bodies, kills them as a people.

There is something about the tyranny of the absolute majority that is really unfair. The dealings with the Indians are one of the most specific examples of this kind of inequity. It is not because they are Indians, or because they are different; it is because there are not enough of them to defend themselves. They are not very strong, and they are sitting on the coal. Or the uranium.

Internment and concentration camps have recently come into national attention because of the media coverage of the internment of the Japanese during World War II. Everyone who looked Japanese was locked up in concentration camps. There were some differences. We called them internment camps; the Germans called them concentration camps. We didn't kill them; but what we did to them was so over-powering and intimidating that they did not begin to complain for twenty or thirty years. They were taken down the streets in chains, ripped off their farms, stuck in camps with all kinds of people they didn't know, on the accident of having the same color skin.

It took the Japanese years before their young people, who weren't so cowed by it, started to speak out.

Now, at this very time, there are Cubans interned in Arkansas; there are Haitians interned in Florida; there are El Salvadoreans interned in Texas; there are Mexicans interned in Texas; and we are talking about moving nine or ten thousand Navajos to somewhere that they don't want to live, which is once again an internment.

They say, "How were the Germans supposed to know about the Jews?"

The same way we are supposed to know about the Navajos, the El Salvadoreans and Haitians and Cubans.

That's the kind of tyranny a majority can get into.

The Indians say that they don't derive their sovereignty from this government. And it is plain to me that they don't. They shouldn't have to; they don't want to. In the U.N. charter it says nobody shall be made a citizen against his will. But the Indians were declared citizens by an act of Congress.

The Reagan administration's moves concerning the environment show this mentality at work. The appointment of Watt to Secretary of Interior is exactly the same kind of place the United States was in during the frontier period: when they got overcrowded, they could just open up a new territory and move on across the continent. They spoke of

198

Manifest Destiny. Now they have bounced off the West Coast, and gone up to Alaska and Hawaii. Now there is no place to go. That argument is now turned around, moving past the nineteenth century imperatives, and is trying to gobble up anything that may have missed destruction the first time through. Watt is appointed to see to the opening up of the territories, with the national forests and the Indian reservations at the top of the hit list.

Russell Means says they aren't really capitalists; because if they were capitalists, they wouldn't be spending the capital.

Few Americans realize that there have been armed confrontations between government authorities and Indians on their own land in the United States and Canada in 1980 and 1981, over questions of raw materials and treaty rights.

At the same time that the Lakota were engaged in armed struggle with the FBI and the BIA at Jumping Bull Camp in 1975, an eighth of that reservation was bartered away for mining rights. And now at the time of the relocation of the Dine people, the Navajo and the Hopi, once again there are mineral rights to be considered. Once again, something that was obviously cooked up in a rich, air conditioned office is going to make a material difference in the lives of thousands of people—there are nine or ten thousand people scheduled to be removed by the government. We watch this country do that to the Indians for no other reason than that Indians don't have any political clout, which is to say they are small in number and can't fight back very well. People may think I'm a radical because I go in friendship and solidarity with the American Indians. But if I am any sort of a regional person, I am a southwesterner; and I and all of my friends when I was a kid wished that the pony soldiers and the cavalry had been better to the Indians, because a lot of our friends were Indians.

That's an American protest. That's not a Russian protest. That's a protest from someone who was raised on Zane Grey.

An Unseen Accuser
And a Midnight Knock

The last time I was on the Teddy Bart Noon Show in Nashville after the amazing raid of 1980, he asked me if in my next book I would tell them about whether we really had the grass or not. It hadn't occurred to me to put that information in the book, about what had happened on 7/11/1980, but I think the people of Nashville and the people of Tennessee have a right to know what went down in their name, inasmuch as, according to a public statement by a Tennessee state legislator, the raid probably cost ten thousand dollars.

The helicopter came down on the afternoon of the tenth. A big old jet-powered Huey, a big noisy chopper, comes close to the ground, going whup, whup, whup, whup. They were so close down on us that we all ran in for our cameras and were immediately out taking pictures of this 'copter on which no markers or numbers could be ascertained from the ground. Of course, we thought that no one would have the nerve to fly an unmarked vehicle except the law.

We watched them fly around over us and apparently go back and refuel and come back and fly around us for a while longer, all afternoon.

Then, in the evening when the crews who worked in Columbia and Nashville were returning to The Farm, word began to trickle in the gate of a massive marshaling of men and equipment at the Maury County Airport. Police cars, four-wheel drive vehicles. We began to be morally certain that we were due for a raid.

We sat and waited. What else could we do?

Late that night, perhaps eleven-thirty, the helicopter returned, and we all knew this was it. I immediately jumped into my clothes and went out to the Gate, meeting several other elders and Farm residents, including our attorney, just as the helicopter came and landed in a field near the front of The Farm, about half a mile from the Gate.

A long line of police cars, led by the Attorney General—highway patrol, local police, television cars from Nashville—stopped at our Gate. The TBI agent handed our lawyer a warrant, and then, to our complete and utter mystification, sped off down the side road past our neighbor's house, instead of asking us to open the gate for them to enter.

We saw the cars bumping over the rutted county road, headlights flashing through the trees, lighting up the helicopter sitting in our melon patch.

I asked the TBI agent who was talking, who seemed to be in charge, if it was all right for me, here on our own farm, to go see what the officers were doing.

Now the warrant for this particular raid, which moved, we are told, some fifty carloads of cops, four-wheel-drive vehicles, dogs, helicopters, all on double time and overtime, in the middle of the night, was a warrant which listed my name alone and gave the right to search the entire Farm. It specified one particular field and then, in quite broad language, opened the search to all adjacent areas and outbuildings. A hundred thirty households stood behind a single name and a single warrant.

I will stop here just parenthetically and let you know that it is the opinion of most of the respectable law in Tennessee that that warrant was no good. That warrant was so bad that government lawyers sent word to me, called me up, sent messages to me by friends, and told me, "That warrant is no good." It is not just my opinion; it is the opinion of a pretty good consensus of the Tennessee legal community.

Well, we didn't have any reefer growing on The Farm. They searched us all night and into the morning. They searched us everywhere they wanted to. We weren't growing any reefer on The Farm.

I questioned the officers as to where in the world did they have the probable cause and authority to have a search warrant issued when they were so wrong. Their story was that someone had been to The Farm and said that we had been growing ten acres of reefer on The Farm, and that we had forced these visitors to work in the marijuana fields. I know this sounds insane, but this was back a year closer to Jonestown days, and people were willing to believe crazy things.

That explains why they thought they could get a warrant. I don't even believe that story; but that is what they said to me about why they could get a warrant.

In the morning, after driving every road on The Farm until it petered out into the woods, and searching the field in question out into its corners, and being unable to find one leaf, one twig, one seed of marijuana, the entire crew loaded back up into their four-wheel-drive vehicles, state trooper cars, sheriff's cars, television cars, Attorney General's cars, and left our property and pulled off, as I had said to the TBI agent,

"You get to serve your warrant. You get to look. And then you have to leave." And they had to leave.

To me, this was the end of it. But I saw the television reports the next day, and saw the police walk away and try to say that we were tipped off, had somehow disappeared ten acres of marijuana in the middle of the night so cleanly and swiftly that not a shred or a trace could be found by the morning's bright light. We were not cleared.

I have many criticisms of how the Tennessee law enforcement people operated on this occasion. They used very questionable practices, I say, such as when retired Agent Ambrose Moss went on the Teddy Bart show as a retiring top Tennessee narc, and made remarks that The Farm was pretty smart and that we had probably gotten rid of the grass before they got to us. That was some of the treatment we received. Ambrose Moss was not on the raid; anything he said was hearsay. I believe he got to go on television and say that after he was retired so he was not technically a member of the TBI anymore, and wouldn't get the TBI in trouble for his statement.

I called every Tennessee law enforcement agency that I knew; I called the FBI; I called Senators Howard Baker and Jim Sasser; I called Congressman Al Gore; I called Speaker of the House Ned McWherter; I called the Attorney General of Tennessee, William Leech, Jr. I called everyone, who would talk to me, and I asked them all the same question:

"If the ones who raided The Farm can walk away and say that the grass was there after they tried every way they knew to prove it was there and could not, how does The Farm have recourse to clear its name?"

I want to clarify a point right here, because the main reason I care about this is our relationship with our Tennessee neighbors. The point in question is not whether hippies smoke grass if they get a chance; we are talking about growing ten acres of grass, a commercial quantity in a poor county where there are unemployed neighbors. If the Attorney General's statement were true, it would mean that we were trafficking in immense amounts of money, a breach of faith with our local neighbors. This mattered to us, whether the TBI understood it or not.

Someone like me with long hair doesn't have much recourse when something like that happens to them. We sued the Attorney General for ten million dollars and a truckload of watermelons; but the people of Tennessee didn't understand the nature of the suit; they thought somehow the state of Tennessee was being attacked, and that they as taxpayers were the ones being sued for this ten million dollars. That was not the case. It was a specific suit against those people we felt had spoken untruth about us: Elmer Davies; Arzo Carson.

Rather than be in a relationship with the people of Tennessee where they think we're trying to get ten million dollars out of them, when we don't even take welfare, we dropped our case. It had been mostly to try to get their attention, anyway.

What I want you to do as a reader at this point is to really try to put yourself in the position of someone who cannot trust the duly constituted, lawfully appointed officials of the state. If they would go away and tell that strong a lie, how can we trust them when we have trouble? To whom can we turn, if we need protection from the law?

I contend that for them not to be men enough to say they were wrong and made a mistake is an act that attempted to outlaw an entire group of people.

I actually hadn't intended to bring this up in a book. But Teddy came on to me on television like,

"Didn't you fox them? Didn't you really have it?"

No, we didn't fox them. No, we really didn't have it. Somebody told a lie, and the result which came to us was an unseen accuser and a midnight knock.

The Christians and the Lions

There is a level of religious discourse going on all over the world, but especially in the United States. In its most simplistic form, it assumes that scientists are not religious, and that anything a scientist says that contradicts the Bible is an attack upon the existence of God. For some reason scientists are assumed to have a vested interest in proving that there is no God. Proving that there is no God is a funny idea. They say in philosophy that it is bad tactics to try to prove a negative.

Can God make a rock bigger than He can lift? The trouble with that one is that God is the rock, God is the maker, God is the lifter, God is the act of lifting, God is the question. There is nothing but God. What else is there? It is not that there is God and there is this other substance, *dreck* or something. It is all God. Madalyn Murray O'Hair, in the Supreme Court, arguing against the teaching of religion in school, is God, as is her argument, and the court, and the schools, and the children.

Sometimes the question hinges on whether God will, from somewhere else outside of the manifestation, reach into the manifestation and make the manifestation do something against its own rules. That is basically what a proof of the existence of God asks. But there is no place outside of the manifestation; the inside and the outside of the manifestation are both equally God; and if *anything* happens in the manifestation, it is the will of God, whether the will of God is that somebody levitates or that somebody does not levitate, or that there are laws of the Universe that seem to preclude levitation.

Our scientists in their telescopes are looking at *fossil light*. They are looking at a light source that is so old that it has burned out millions of years ago; the light from it is just now getting to us, and that light source no longer exists. But even out on the other side of where that fossilized light came from, it is still one place with this. Also, that piece of fossilized light has been shining the other way, too; and however long it has been going this way, it has also been going *that* way. And over there is one place with this place. So God is obviously all in one place. This is it.

Pantheists say that God is in everything, and that when the crow makes the crow sound, that is God speaking through that crow, who they might say was the crow god, or the bird god or the animal god. When a big rock cliff freezes and thaws for thousands of years so that it finally cracks loose the last little support that was holding it to the rest of the cliff, and a big chunk of it crumbles away through no human action, and falls, they say the rock god, who lives in the rock, let go. The pantheists say that everything has God in it. The monotheists say that everything does not have God in it, that God is in a central location, and communicates out to all those places.

Just after the Russian revolution, many Russian patriots felt that they had been forced by the church to give themselves up to the tsar, felt that the church was the most enslaving influence in Russian culture. The serfs had been compelled to accept the idea that the tsar had divine right, and that the tsar's deputies, all the nobility and courtiers, all had divine right, and that it was God's plan that the serfs should live in poverty and have to work for the nobility for nothing, and be owned by the nobility. It was God's plan, because the tsar had divine right; God had ordained that he be the king, and that these peasants be dirt.

So, at the end of the revolution, when the peasants got to do what they wanted to do, they were not philosophers or intellectuals; but they knew that *they did not want that to happen to them again.* They said they'd had a lot of pie-in-the-sky dumped on them, and that they wanted to prove that there was no such thing as pie in the sky. They had museums where people who had been to the ends of the earth came back and said they did not find God. When they had airplanes, they had statements from Russian pilots who had flown very high and had not found heaven. Later on, the Russian astronauts sent their statements down to this museum, that there was no God. I wonder what they did with the Russian astronauts who got stoned, like ours did, and came back all religious feeling and mind-blown. Probably figured out how to shut them up.

Atheism is not the real statement of the Russian people. It is a political statement by a small political group who wanted to ensure that the serfs would not fall under the control of anyone through misuse of religion. It was sort of a reminder, like Wonder Woman's bracelets. Wonder Woman wears bracelets around her wrists to remind her that if she ever allows a man to put a chain between those bracelets, she will lose all her powers.

Russian people meet in basements with guards posted at the door to have services. Russian Jews are just assumed to be political. They are locked up, put away, denied permission to leave the country, on the basis that the state is not religious, and is against the people being religious. But the people of Russia are not godless.

A lot of religion, especially Christianity, has fallen into what the Catholics called, many years ago, the Manichean heresy. The Manichees were a religious group who operated on the idea that God was a force, and that the devil was a force, that they were at war, and that the outcome was in doubt. The Catholic Church excommunicated the Manichees because they said that, when you are running a prayer/magic/religious/telepathic show, in the first place, you do not presume your own loss, because your presumptions help determine the outcome. If you're going to be in *this* club, you assume that it is all one thing. It says so in the Bible: the sun

209

and the rain and the dark and the light..."I, the Lord, do all these things." *All* these things.

It is now taught by the *evangelicos*, the fifty-million-dollar-a year television preachers, that God has opinions about how we live down to very subtle levels: that God cares whether we have government taking care of the people or supply-side economics; that God cares whether we have a multiple-re-entry-vehicle ballistic missile or an MX system in the Utah desert.

God is a communist. God is a fascist. God is a Jew. God is a Christian. God is a hippy.

The central problem with the Manichean heresy is the idea that the system is so wrong, that the manifestation is so wrong that God must, from some outside position, reach inside the manifestation and change it from its own laws or it is not good enough. This is the error. The truth is that goodness of heart counts. People who are not too severely oppressed will come to just ideas. Justice is such a common idea that we will all have ideas of justice if we are simply not so oppressed that we are not allowed to. The idea of justice is recognizable from person to person. Love is recognizable from person to person. No matter how many generations it takes, no matter how much the cost, the good intelligence that we pass down and the love and clearness of heart and kindness and care and tolerance and humorous intelligence that we bring with us from generation to generation is inexorable, and is of itself enough to carry us through. That is recognizable above language, above culture, above religion. Love and justice *will prevail*, and the heresy is to think otherwise.

Here is a problem in creation: Which came first, the chicken or the egg?

That is a riddle that people have popped on each other for generations. It seems like it ought to have an answer, but it almost doesn't seem to when you examine it. The reason it doesn't really have an answer is that, to accept that riddle as something to think out, you have to presuppose that the chicken or the egg, either one, came into being *Pop!* all at

210

once. When we said chickens and eggs, we didn't necessarily say chicken eggs. That's why the question doesn't work, because it didn't happen that way. There ought to be an alternate answer, because it did happen. We have chickens, and eggs. There must be some process by which this happened.

There is no logical reason why one should have preceded the other, if they both came into being *Pop!* all at once. But if you have been looking at the rocks for a while, you will notice that chickens are merely one of a class of egg layers, and the class of egg layers is much older than chickens. Obviously, eggs came before chickens.

That is a problem about creation whose problematic nature stemmed from the assumption about it.

Problems about creation plague all good philosophers. My son Paul, when he was four or five, said,

"Was all this stuff already here, or did it have to get here?"

When you get to something as universal as, "When did the Creation start," you are stuck with *how* did the Creation start, and who started it, what started it, what was there before it was there, if it had to start, and you're just stuck right into Philosophy 1-A. There's nothing you can do about it, once you accept that question.

Another one of those is, "Did the Universe come into being and then generate spirit and consciousness, or did consciousness and spirit pre-exist the Creation?"

What's wrong with that one is that it assumes that consciousness, creation, and spirit, are separate, or can be separated. The old Indians used to say that once the salt was in the water, you couldn't get it back out. But that's not true. You can just boil it down and scrape the salt off the bottom of the pan. But consciousness and creation aren't like that.

The Catholic credo says world without end, time without stop.

When Paul asked that question, he made another assumption. He made an assumption about himself when he wanted to know about "this stuff." Rene Descartes, the French philosopher, is well-known for his saying, *Cogito ergo sum,* which is Latin for *I think, therefore I am*. Or, "Here I am. I just noticed myself." Aldous Huxley, another philosopher of impeccable credentials, said, *Eructo ergo sum*, which means, *I belch, therefore I am*. He was trying to put the question of existence where it belongs: in existing, rather than in thinking about existing.

Here we are. We exist. Anything we say about existence and creation is tempered by that fact. We know the stories of creation of a great many cultures. The Sun God dipped his samurai sword into the ocean and dug it into the mud of the bottom, and dragged his sword back out of the water. The mud dripped off his samurai sword, and it was the Japanese islands.

The answer to all those problems and all those questions is that the creator, the creation, and the act of creating are all one. The creator, which is to say the side of the creation that you would split apart if you were to say, *And then God made earth* or *God made the Universe*, is the same as the earth part but it isn't split apart.

The act of creation, whether a big bang, or whatever universal theory, is one with the creator, and one with the creation.

The knower, the act of knowing, and the knowledge are one.

We are one with God. We have no choice. You don't really have to worry about being one with God: there aren't any other options.

The creation stories of the old time folks had to do with how big a world view they had. They would say, "Before my father's time, or before grandfather's time, or before great-grandfather's time, or before the time of the oldest history that we had, was creation."

Through the organized system of our observations over a period of years and generations, we have derived a certain set of information which we provisionally believe to be the actual facts. The reason we say provisionally is that we have been keeping track long enough to notice that the facts seem to slide a little bit every couple of generations, as we learn more things.

According to that body of knowledge, which has its own ethical code called the scientific method, we have been able to push back our knowledge about how long all this has been here, farther and farther, especially in the last fifty years. Previously, our methods of dating depended primarily on the layers of mud we were digging in, and the nature of what we found in it. If you dug down through layers and layers of mud over a period of time, and found that you were down layers and layers that had to be thousands and thousands of years old, and you found certain creatures as you went down through it, you would have a tendency to think you were seeing creatures from succeeding ages.

Some of the rock they were looking at apppeared to be just like it was made originally, plain old earth stuff. Other kinds seemed to have been weathered down, broken down, meshed together, put deep in the earth and heated up, compressed together, and made into a great variety of stuff. And the layers and patterns of that also have certain clues in them as to their antiquity.

That was the state of the art about fifty years ago. Then we began to be able to make assumptions about the age of things by how quickly radioactive substances break down.

The Fundamentalists question radiocarbon or potassium dating as a method of dating. If the scientific establishment isn't smart enough to do radiocarbon dating, how can you trust them with nuclear power?

On one end, radiocarbon dating is keyed to the half life of Carbon-14. On the other end, it is keyed to the charcoal from trees with rings which can be identified historically. All the trees of a region will have the same rainfall patterns, and you can determine age from tree rings. They have overlapping tree rings traveling back thousands and thousands of years. Radiocarbon dating is hooked up to things in recent enough history that you calibrate it on tree rings and radiocarbon dating together. It is not conjecture.

Since we have been observing the creation, we have developed certain ideas about patterns we see running through the way it behaves, until we have organized it in classifications and categories. Furthermore, the way it behaves seems to bear out these classifications and categories, not only to the point of making all of the elements logical in their sequence but also to be able to predict that, according to this pattern, certain other elements, hitherto undiscovered, ought to exist. Through the atomic age, we have discovered other elements and even fundamental subatomic particles, having predicted in advance that they should exist.

This is getting down to a pretty fine shading of the knowledge. It has to do with the periodic table of elements, and the way in which the patterns of their atomic weight can be discerned even in their gross characteristics. For example, gold, silver, and copper are all in one column. Another category that lines up like that is the gases, argon, neon, xenon, krypton.

In the early days of anthropology and archeology, they thought the beginnings of mankind were fifty or seventy-five thousand years ago in Europe. They talked about the Cro-Magnons and the Neanderthals. As they studied that, they have found that some very intelligent two-leggeds who used tools and act like people as far as we can tell from this distance, looking back at them, intelligent tool-users, have been around for perhaps a million years. Something very much like humankind has been around for a *very long time*.

We find the records of their actions printed in the soil where they live. We find a place where they start using fire, by radiocarbon dating stuff that has been burnt. It's like looking at a circle of light. You can strike a match, and see how big a circle you can see. You can build a fire, and see a much bigger circle. Now, we have built a pretty big light, and we have built a *huge* circle. And you know what?

No edges.

We haven't found any edges yet. No edges.

When I say the creator, the creation and the act of creating are one, that piece of philosophy is from *The Upanishads*, some of the oldest writings we have. Those writings don't think the world began five thousand years ago; because those writings were written twelve thousand years ago.

When it began, if it began, is irrelevant, because it is happening now, it is beginning now. It has always been beginning, because the act of creation, the beginning, and the creation, the existing, and the creator, are all one. There is no question in there and it, too, is only another apparent riddle.

This argument about evolution or creation actually was developed in the early 1900's in the United States. The argument that has come down to us is based on the level of anthropological and scientific knowledge that was available then. What I find is that, if you look at state-of-the-art science and state-of-the-art religion, not just true believers of either branch, but ones who are *really good* on both sides, what you find is a statement like that of Albert Einstein, the father of modern physics, who said the farther he got into science the more religious he got, the more he knew there was God. He said that something so fine, without end, and immaculately perfect in its own laws, made him religious the longer he studied it.

The argument between the creationists and the evolutionists has not even been joined. The reason the question has not been joined is that no spokesman has come up, who was an educated religious person, to talk with a fundamentalist. The argument has been with someone like Carl Sagan, who's an agnostic, however high his feelings may be at some times.

I have had religious experiences. I am a religious person. I *understand* the divinity of Jesus, and am at peace with it. But I do not grant exclusivity; and this is where the battle is joined, at John 3:16, which contains the line, "Only begotten Son". This is central to the Christian doctrine, the question of *begotten*, which is to say that through some agency or other, the Creator impregnated a mortal. For this, Paul and the dogmatists claim a special son-ship for Jesus.

In what he said, Jesus was obviously trying to be not a moat, but a bridge. He is not trying to be an insurmountable obstacle between humanity and God. He said, "You are all sons of God." He Himself did not make any issue of the question of begotten-ness.

To me, Father, Son and Holy Ghost means the Creator, First Cause, Primal Entity, not even in the Universe because there is no Universe; the Universe is contained within it; the Son is those creatures which have evolved, under God's clean Law, to a place where they attempt to understand God, which is the godliness of humankind; and the Holy Ghost which is the non-space-time spiritual medium in which all of the dichotomies may be resolved, all of the space and time questions may be resolved, all of the eternity/instant questions may be resolved, all of the prophecy questions may be resolved, because of this absolute non-space-time-ness.

That which follows God's Law is part of God, and is divinely created. From the evidence of science, which is nothing more than the body of our observations within the framework of the scientific method, timebound over a period of years, by communication, our observation seems to be that God is expressed on earth through clear evidence which we are able to see, of change from age to age. It is not an affront to man to say that people are part of God's animal creation. People obviously have a quality which the animals do not have: the quality of free thought, free will, memory, plan. A lion kills because it was created by its circumstances, which we could call God, to do so. Man has a choice about whether to kill or not. Man has a choice about everything. If there was a place where evolution would ever stop, it would be where man took control of himself. Man hasn't changed for the environment; he's changed the environment to fit him. Man is an evolutionary force.

The question becomes foggy around the idea of the timespans required to give free play to an evolutionary force.

Fundamentalists say "The Jews have been cutting the foreskins off of babies for the last five thousand years, and babies are still not born without foreskins."

Besides being offensive, this is a side argument in the question. The Fundamentalists have not been into it deeply

216

enough to recognize that there is a discussion going on between Lysenkoism and Western thought on the question of evolution. There is a difference between evolution as preached in the Soviet Union and in the United States. In the west, we do not assume that acquired traits are inherited; but the Russians assumed, and this is called the Lysenkoan heresy, that acquired characteristics are passed on.

Lysenko was a great Russian biologist. He got bent by the state on the question of whether acquired characteristics are inherited. He said they were. Western science does not agree with that, and considers that a perversion forced on the Russian biologists by the State, who taught that the giraffe reaches for the leaf and the baby giraffe is born with a longer neck.

The Fundamentalists have not been following this argument all these years. The Lysenko-Western argument knocks a lot of the legs out of the Fundamentalists' position, because their arguments assume the Lysenkoan heresy in all evolutionary thought; that's one of the reasons they can't stand it; because it isn't standable at that point.

They aren't deep enough into the argument to learn what's going on because they're taking theirs out of the book. Their question is not about evolution; their question is about the divinely inspired nature of the Bible, all of it. To defend the divinely inspired nature of the Bible, all of it, they have to defend the divinely inspired nature of the Council of Worms of 1530-something, and the divinely inspired nature of every editorial board and crew that worked on translating it and editing it; the King James guys who translated it out of the Greek; all these guys have to be considered and created as special agents of God in order to have a completely divinely inspired Bible all the way through.

If you programmed a Bible into a computer and asked it to cancel itself, you'd reduce it by about half. Take out all of the mutually-exclusive statements and choose the one which in your judgment seems best; it might not choose right all the time, but it would be interesting to see what you got. But it would slim down. Because it's written by a lot of different people. The Fundamentalists are assuming a unitary construction of the Bible, which places them as dependent on the Catholics as they can possibly be. The divine inspiration of those guys who edited it, all those times it was edited, all down through history, depends on the Catholics. It's their hierarchy that declared those guys cool to edit it.

The Fundamentalists are working out of the King James, period. They argue that the fact that the book has been handed down for so long is evidence of the divinity of its origin. But it's not the same book. It's changed, every time it was touched, according to dogma at the time. The Catholic Church does not say that the earth is the physical center of the solar system any more. They just can't; it's Flat-Earth, to try to say that. Galileo faced the inquisition for saying they were wrong about that. They can't fight that one right now, because the math is too compelling; the observations all work out. You can dispatch spacecraft across interstellar space on the basis of these calculations and they get there. Galileo got a retroactive pardon.

What gets me is how the folks who are taking political and economic policy out of the Bible and calling it the work of God can justify the ignorance and sloppiness that they presuppose on the part of a scientist on the question of biology and evolution, and still trust nuclear energy, with the amount of precision it requires to make it happen. They tear down that part of science which they don't like, and keep other parts of science on some other grounds.

The idea that the Christian myth of creation is being taught in the schools as of equal validity with all of the observations of science, is an example of a decline in the educational standards of the United States. The electorate cannot, under the present system of education, be properly informed on the question of nuclear power. Nobody did that good in school. Just hardly anybody.

It shows that you can be a lawyer or a doctor, and still be ignorant of other disciplines you haven't studied, and you can believe dumb stuff.

The question about the divinity of the Bible is not whether

or not I consider the Bible to be divinely inspired. The question is, *Does not the Constitution protect the Jews and Zoroastrians from having the story of one religion taught in the schools to mold the minds of all the children in the school?*

There aren't going to be many Christian biologists in the next few decades; they aren't going to be able to pass their courses well enough.

The whole question centers around the Fundamentalists' contention that the Bible is infallible. We have to say that there are other religions in the United States, and the Constitution protects those other religions. Schools belong to the government; and a government agency should not teach the religious teaching of any religion. The schools can teach the basic spiritual values that are common to all religions. Teaching the children to be good, teaching the children to be honest, teaching the children to stay away from bad dope and alcohol, teaching the children not to be promiscuous sexually, can all be done within the school system, and is of equal value to the church and the state; but it cannot be taught, from the viewpoint of a religion—any religion.

The secret of this country has completely been lost by the *evangelicos* and the Moral Majority. The secret is that both atheists *and* religious get to live in this country, and that they don't get to run over each other's feet. There are people who believe in God and people who don't believe in God, people who are Jews and people who are Christians, people who are hippies and people who are Episcopalians and people who are Catholics and people who are Zoroastrians, and anything else, because the agreement we came together under said that Congress would not make a law respecting the establishment of a religion. They aren't supposed to say, "This one's real," "This one's not real." They aren't even supposed to *say* it.

We turn out people who know how to run an adding machine but don't know what makes a tree grow. People who can fix a machine but don't know the principles it works on. We have people now who are spoken of as "electronic technicians", who merely know the catalog of resistors and parts, and can do the math and compute the values of them. Even with the level of information available to the public about almost any subject, the level of education is so bad and the country is so philosophically and scientifically illiterate as a whole, that you no more can answer the questions of nuclear power or evolution with the materials at hand, than the Tennessee level of psychiatry is capable of determining innocence by reason of insanity.

At a sophisticated level of religion, it is a sin to require or teach material proofs. The point of all this is not that I offer to solve the questions of evolution/creationism or nukes/no nukes, although I may have strong opinions on those subjects. Rather, it is that the issues themselves are not true issues, but are symptomatic of the decadent condition of the educational establishment of the United States.

It is not a failure of the educational establishment to keep pace with technology. They tried to use the assembly-line techniques of technology in education, and lost the techniques of transmission and respect for knowledge and education. A lot of people don't have respect for knowledge; the people who have the most respect for knowledge are very common folk.

We have no tradition; that's one of the reasons we're like this. The Fundamentalists are hanging on to a tradition. They're trying to say,

"This is our traditional world view. We do not wish to give up our traditional world view."

No one requires that they give it up; but they aren't defending it well enough to win a high school debate. And they surely cannot be permitted to impose their traditional world view on anybody else's children.

The New Royalty

Americans, for a country that had a long and arduous revolutionary war, have a continuing illicit love affair with royalty. Catholic Americans frequently solicit church nobility—knights of the Church. Even American robber barons sought for the touch of nobility to legitimize their efforts. It is not generally known that Commodore Vanderbilt spent several millions more to purchase a title for his daughter than he did to endow Vanderbilt University. But now the United States has been here long enough that we are beginning to develop our own royalty.

Social position is hereditary. In politics, the proliferation of Longs and Roosevelts, Talmadges and Rockefellers, the number of politicians who are married to the daughters of other politicians, shows that there has been a hereditary ruling class in this country. And now, we have a new generation of hereditary rulers.

It has long been conventional for true nobility to distrust the theater. Actors were not to be trusted; they could learn the right accent and fool you, and be from the wrong social class even if they talked right and looked right. But, in a true American spirit, being from the theater is no longer a social liability; in the spirit of "if you can't lick 'em, join 'em," much of our new royalty is from the entertainment world.

The people who went to Hollywood to join that absolutely new medium of moving pictures and talking pictures came from the soda shops and one-horse garages of the small towns of America, came to Hollywood and became famous and rich, and became the royalty; and now they are the hereditary royalty. Now we see the sons and daughters of the Nelsons, of the Crosbys, of the Carradines, of the Barrymores, becoming the second generation of media royalty.

The son of Mike Wallace works for the other network, but in his father's footsteps.

Americans have always been a little envious of the Europeans and their royalty. It was plain when Nixon put the comic opera uniforms on the White House Guard, that he was a little competitive with Buckingham Palace and the Coldstream Guard. He wanted to look *impressive*.

There is another strong tradition in America which has no use for royalty whatever. Those were the people who laughed heartily on news that the Nixon White House Guard uniforms were sold to a high school band in Texas, where they properly belonged.

These are not merely Constitutional nobility that we speak of, but the actual nobility. Interchangeability ranges among the media. Simon, of Simon and Schuster, has a daughter, Carly, who sings. Ektachrome, Kodak, marries a Beatle: Linda Eastman. America wants any touch of royalty that it can have.

It would be comical to see the lusting after royalty, if it weren't so unconstitutional.

The new royalty are those who are accidentally knighted or coroneted by the media. The new feudalism is the stranglehold of the multinational corporations on the planet. The Fame Game is the institutionalization of the upward mobility of the arts and sports. The new heraldry is designed not by the chroniclers of the genealogies of the noble, but by the commercial artists of the rich.

Indianapolis is another example of the hereditary royalty in the United States. You have a better chance of getting into Indianapolis if your name is Vucovich or Bettenhausen or Unser or any other of several famous family racing names. Pettys in the stock cars. This is the natural tendency, for folks who have access to extend that access on to their kids. The sons of mechanics and moonshiners race with royal and noble playboys on European tracks and live at upper class spas on the circuit.

The royalty has certain perquisites of its position, although they say it isn't so. But it was very plain to see in the recent controversy over *Sixty Minutes'* coverage of a story on Duvalier's regime in Haiti. There had been a story done some time in the past, and the network had determined that it was time for a follow-up story to occur, and the story had been assigned to Morley Safer.

Mike Wallace went to Morley Safer and told him that he had relatives who had a business in Haiti, and he was afraid that the story might cause street violence, and possibly get their business damaged. He asked Morley Safer not to do the story, and Morley Safer agreed. Then the word got out. Wallace had to admit that, yes, he did do that, and he realized that the network had to run the story, that he shouldn't have done it, and that the network was forced to run the story now, because otherwise there was a pretty serious question of whether a national regime could be covered up behind the relatives of one of the reporters. The breach of faith as a newsperson that Mike Wallace committed is half the story. The other half is the use of undelegated power as a member of the hereditary royalty and the ruling oligarchy that can change a national television presentation on an entire country, which is an affair of state, whether Alexander Haig likes it or not.

There is class of diseases called "orphan diseases"—those which have few enough victims as to be non-cost-effective for drug companies to develop a program in their behalf. When some power was brought to bear on Turett syndrome, one of the orphan diseases, it was through Jack Klugman, star of the medical show *Quincy*, a surrogate doctor for media purposes—although his true media power came from being Tony Randall's roommate. He not only did a television story on the Turett syndrome on *Quincy*; but he took the research on the Turett syndrome and a real victim before government hearings and boards, and was one of the power witnesses who was able to get the idea of Turett syndrome and orphan diseases in general before the public eye. Someone who used to be Tony Randall's roommate has been touched with the magic of power until he can become an ombudsman before the government about a subject in which he has had no training except as a media personality.

In the same way, the woman who plays the girl reporter on *Lou Grant* testified at Senate hearings on the breastmilk controversy.

More and more it becomes common for media people to speak before the government—even unto the point of hiring an actor for President.

The perquisites of this modern royalty are real, in exactly the same way that being the Governor-General of Australia is not an empty honorific for Prince Charles. Tremendous amounts of power are concentrated in a few people's hands.

The question of hereditary royalty is going to become a lot more of a personal issue to the people of Tennessee. I see that Howard Baker's daughter is going to run for public office now. That is a perfect example of what in any business would be called nepotism, where, because you have some authority in the business and know the ropes and have a little bit of power, you can arrange for your relatives to get hired. If she actually does run for a public office, her daddy's machine will be at her disposal. That's such a tremendous advantage on anybody else who is running for office that it's almost like being able to hire them.

We see a lot of second generation names in Congress. In a country of over two hundred million people, it is a shame that there are any second generation names in Congress with as many people as there are in the United States who remain unrepresented. That we should have representation for the second and third times for the Long family and the Roosevelts while there are millions and millions of people who are completely unrepresented is clearly unfair.

224

The Pendulum Swings

One of the major flaws in the reasoning of the new right is that there was some time in the past when things were a lot better than they are now. But if you have read the right kind of history books, and you have seen how consistently and how often we have hired the Pinkertons to beat back the unions, you can see that there never was a time when the burning issues of rich and poor, left and right, were not in question. I think Herb Shriner said it best when he said,

"Things ain't like they used to be. And they never was, either."

Many people have become historically and politically sophisticated enough to see that there is a pendulum effect in society, and that when it swings far one way, it will swing the other way in time, to balance. This can be seen not only in the intellectual journals, but in the mass magazines and even the newspapers.

The effect on society of the media, once again is a kind of speed other than chemical or mechanical. Just before John Mitchell went to jail over Watergate, he said,

"This country's going to go so far right so fast you wouldn't recognize it."

It was on its way. It was slowed down and temporarily turned around by Watergate. But as soon as Watergate evaporated, the massive tendency of the pendulum, which was in reaction against the radicalism of the 'sixties, reasserted itself and took the country, just as Mitchell said, farther right than we would ever have believed.

We cannot assume, or allow ourselves to be panicked into believing that that temporary poised position at the far right is the end of the American experiment that has gone on these two hundred years. The pendulum is going to come back, and faster than last time.

The effect of the media is to make millions of people aware within hours or days of any significant political event. When the Constitution was signed, it was months before the people of the country affected by it knew about it completely, and it was years before it was known around the world. With modern media, we watch the fall of deposed dictators in slow motion, like football quarterbacks collapsing before an onrushing line. Under the influence of the huge amounts of mass opinion that can be moved in the twentieth century, the pendulum can move fast. This is not the first time we have been in this position, and this is not the last time we are going to be in this position in our lives; but we have a grave necessity to understand that damping the movement of the pendulum is more important than pushing it to one side or the other.

The crazinesses where ordinary people get hurt occur under fast and ill-considered decisions.

The swinging of the pendulum itself is a state of flux. As this state of flux cools, our society will be like a super-saturated solution, and the kind of crystals that the media seed in the minds of the people will be a major factor in determining what kind of a world it settles into being.

It is strange to think we are reduced to these kinds of straits, but it is significant that Alan Alda is a better television producer than Jerry Falwell, and it matters.

The United States went into a very rigid and controlled and militaristic attitude in the country during World War II to get the economy together in order to face the Nazis. That caused a repression and an economic move at the same time. After the war, they talked about the postwar housing, the postwar cars. After the war people wanted to be free. People who had been all for military discipline wanted to have a free civilian life. The people began swinging toward liberal things and it got really strong during the 'sixties when it was at the extreme end of the swing. At that time the pendulum had swung so extremely in one direction that it scared the other extreme. There were people making love in the streets. It was wild and woolly and a little scary to some folks.

At that moment began the seeds of the swing to the other direction. When Nixon was elected this swing was going right wing fast. Mitchell was watching the protesters being hauled away without the benefit of proper arrest papers and herded into a football field. The swing to the right was coming of larger things than Watergate, which only slowed it down. Now they're putting back together the same team. They're sticking in Alexander Haig, they're taking information from Nixon. They're taking information from Kissinger. They're putting in Rumsfeld and all these old Nixon guys.

I think that the seeds of the swing back the other way have already happened. I think the seeds of the swing back the other way began when Reagan made it plain that he was going to stick the same administration back down on us. The people remembered Vietnam; people remembered Watergate. Reagan became identified to everyone as merely the front man for that same old team that was the power behind Nixon and people began to realize that Reagan was not the new beginning after all.

Other things happened that bred cynicism. The Moral Majority who had just finished putting all their energy into electing Ronald Reagan, gave press conferences about, if he isn't right wing enough we'll get rid of him and get one that is.

People are beginning to be outraged by the attitudes toward Guatemala and El Salvador and the amount of American guns involved in that conflict. Ambassador Kirkpatrick says "Well the thing we didn't do in El Salvador was we didn't send down helicopters soon enough." These things are outraging the United States. There must be 25 or 50 million people in this country who were touched so strong

by the 'sixties that they will never be the same again.
History becomes important. We have to educate the young
folks who are stepping into the middle of something that's
already moving. If they understand how it's already moving
they can be like a jujitsu player and they can move with the
inertia of the times. If they don't know what's happening, if
they think it's the first time around for them and this is all a
new movie and don't realize about the periodicities, they're
not going to be able to move with this great movement.

The conservatives think that people who are on welfare are
somehow bad, evil, at fault, wrong or cheats. This attitude,
transferred into government, produces Reagan's statement
that we will not be carrying on Mr. Carter's emphasis on
human rights in our foreign policy. Then it moves to the
Secretary of State saying that this administration will not be
centering on human rights, but on the eradication of
terrorism. It falls down the chain of command to the police
chief of Memphis who advises the castration of rapists, and
to the police chief of Nashville, Joe Casey, who advises
capital punishment and public execution for a variety of
offenses never before considered to be capital crimes. It leads
directly to excusing some kinds of violence—such as against
gays or blacks—while multiplying the punishments for
crimes against *property*.

The current atmosphere of crackdown and never mind the
civil rights, get the criminals off the street, is a perfect
example of how the work of one administration can be
destroyed by the next administration. Many states, including
Tennessee, have what is called the Habitual Criminal Act. It
says that if you are busted for four felonies—heavy crimes,
that you can be called a habitual criminal, and you can get
life in prison for that.

The Habitual Criminal Act has been misinterpreted. Suppose someone does a criminal act, perhaps selling heroin on
the street. He gets busted, goes to trial, is sentenced in court,
goes to jail, then gets out of jail and does it again, is busted,
tried, sentenced and back in jail. Now if he does it two more
times, he is called a habitual criminal.

What is currently going on in the court system in Tennessee is that some attorneys general and police are interpreting the law to mean that if they put a stakeout on you and they watch you sell dope on Monday, and then they watch you sell dope on Tuesday, and then they watch you sell dope on Wednesday, that when you sell dope on Thursday, that you have committed all four of your convictions in one hit, and from being monitored doing a criminal act four days in a row, you can be named a habitual criminal, and you can be put in jail for life for a series of minor offenses.

It is obvious that what is missing in this scenario is the chance for someone to be warned by their first punishment and straighten up. The people trying to use the law like that are not going to succeed; it will cause too much inequity. We have already seen the inequity of this kind of thinking in Texas, where there is a man in jail under the habitual criminal act for four felonies which add up to a total of two hundred eighty-nine dollars. Among his four felonies were included such crimes as writing a hot check for the rent. Now they are trying to make it so you don't even have to have a separate offense, or a separate trial, or a separate occasion.

This is an unfair treatment, and an unfair treatment causes criminals to feel justified.

I saw where a Nashville criminal court judge said that the Tennessee system of dealing out punishment is so capricious as to be unfair. I was grateful to see someone in the establishment mention that, because one of the most significant things I learned on my trip through the penitentiary system was the capriciousness of sentencing.

The only reason anybody ever gets the right amount of time for the amount of crime they did is the same reason that a stopped clock is right twice a day. Other than that, there is no reason for it to match up. You see guys who kill people and get thirteen months. You see guys who kill people and get fifty years. You see guys who kill people and get three hundred years.

The system of pardons and paroles is not too good

currently. I believe people in Tennessee are aware of how it was when pardons and paroles were being bought and sold by the government wholesale. But the real cause of the capriciousness and injustice of the sentencing system is that there is an open, tacit lie going on between the corrections department, the enforcement department, the judicial department, and the legislative department.

Anybody who is in law enforcement or corrections, immediately upon hearing the amount of time associated with a particular crime, translates that into real time. We have two kinds of time: jury time, which is to pacify the people who were the victims of the crime and the members of the community who were offended by the crime. Jury time is very high. Then we have the amount of time that it is possible or practical to give anyone in the reality of a severely overcrowded prison system, which cannot possibly take everyone who is in it now with all the lengths of time they were given. If all the people in the pen had to serve the exact amount of time that they were convicted for, it would double and triple and quadruple the amount of time being served, which would double and triple and quadruple the prison population. It is impossible to sustain it. They know they cannot sustain it. Corrections knows that putting long periods of time on people for minor crimes in the first place is not a deterrent, and in the second place clogs the system. Corrections knows that a short sentence that comes on sure is more pragmatic and cost-effective and rehabilitation-effective for society. And the policemen who have been in law enforcement for any period of time know that. They know how much trouble they are getting someone in when they write him up. They know what the average real-life sentence is, never mind what it says cosmetically.

Not only is the amount of time capricious in this fashion, but different people have interest group reasons for making there be more time, other than anything functional. Legislators think it makes them look tough to pass laws advising a lot of time. Legislators can go back to their constituents saying,

"Hey, look how much time we're going to give them for this crime."

Attorneys General know that it looks good for them, it looks like they were effective lawyers if they get a lot of time on the people they prosecute. So Attorneys General always go for the max.

Then, in Tennessee, with that much special interest group involved in it already, we have the legal structure and custom where the juries can set the sentences, so an emotional lawyer can move a jury to give someone more time than anybody in the legal system ever thinks they're going to serve.

The Parole Board thinks another thing.

This system, since it is such a badly structured system, allows a lot of slop in the form of undelegated power laying around, because the right people who are supposed to have the power are not using it properly. The judges, lawyers and attorneys general are in cahoots to have several standards of sentencing, because they get to move around in the system in the form of plea bargaining, where you offer someone the real time, and tell them they'll get jury time if they don't hurry up and confess or plead guilty. The Attorney General can say,

"All right, I'm going to ask for the max. Not only that, I'm going to have the jury sentence you and ask for the max. If you don't like that, you can plead guilty and you'll only get ten or twenty years, instead of life."

This isn't just Tennessee. These abuses and many others actually exist throughout the United States in various forms, allowing for local law. On one side we have the libraries full of law books that it takes to balance and maintain such an inequitable and sloppy system; but in the penitentiary, most of the lore can go on a few proverbs.

"If you can't stand the time, don't do the crime."

Previous to the penitentiary, there was no such thing as criminals. People learn to be criminals in the penitentiary. They may do some personal act of greed or stupidity that lands them in the pen; but they aren't criminals yet. The pen makes them into criminals. A criminal is someone who is "in the club" against the law. A convict will mostly team up along with any other convict against the heat.

It's a very tight club, being a good con. That's where they create people who work together to do larger crimes; they are educated in the pen.

It was either my mother or my grandmother who told me, "There are lies, damn lies, and statistics."

Statistics can be used to prove a lot of things. Some of the great national issues right now have statistics being used by both sides, and each side's statistics appear to be true. On one hand, a large segment of society says it's about time we rooted out white collar crime, that the public is defrauded and ripped off of literally billions of dollars in white collar crime. At the same time, the administration tells us it doesn't think the people are very concerned about white collar crime, because it only takes a few dollars apiece from each of them. What the government says they think the public is worried about is robbery or violent crime, where individuals give up a lot.

These are different sociological viewpoints. Their viewpoint is that, because the victims individually are more disturbed about being robbed with a gun than they are about being robbed through government and business collusion, it is the government's obligation to root out this crime by longer sentences, harsher penalties, stiffer fines, speedier trials.

This is a case where the statistical answer is quite justified. The situation of an individual victim of crime is much like the question of the infant mortality rate in the birth of children. When one experiences the births of many children, a large enough number that the statistics come into play, it is known that you are going to lose one sometimes. There are statistics put out by hospitals that indicate that losing ten per thousand is considered okay, even good, in delivering babies. But it is completely unacceptable to those ten sets of parents. Completely. They are not consoled by the knowledge that they are only one of ten per thousand.

It is the same way with the crime statistics. Each of the

crimes, as presented, is unacceptable both to the victim and as a social phenomenon, *although the statistics predicted it.*

In order to determine what is actually happening, you have to look at the statistical picture of crime. The statistical picture of crime can be related directly to the statistics of the economy and money, the statistics of social factors. It can be shown that as certain other large social factors rise and fall, so does crime rise and fall; and although the individual crimes are inexcusable as crimes in the way that births are unacceptable as deaths, they are sociologically caused. To attack the crime rate is to move in at the direction of education, social programs, decent living, care of neighborhoods so that families can have a decent life. If your family is in a bomb zone or a war zone, you cannot have a decent life, whoever you are. The administration's policies are shortsighted and, instead of reducing social unrest by cracking down, they cause it.

As soon as Reagan's stance became well known, some sixty days into his administration—as seen in the kind of funds he cut, the kinds of countries he sent foreign aid to, the people he backed, his attitudes and who his friends were—we saw the Klan come on strong and making a lot more noise than it had been making. We saw the beating up of gay people in San Francisco and all over the United States becoming more and more acceptable, with the gay people having less and less recourse to law.

The effects of President Reagan's and Secretary of State Haig's policies are also easy to see in the United States itself. Paramilitary groups arm themselves and indulge in combat training, not just in Alabama and Mississippi, but Florida, upstate New York, Southern California, Arizona and New Mexico; not just the Ku Klux Klan, but Jewish paramilitary groups, black paramilitary groups. It becomes apparent that a climate of violence is being tolerated in the United States.

Other countries in the world consider the violence and gunmania in the United States to be pathological. They consider us to be a sick society. Americans who go to Europe are frequently asked,

"Are you from Chicago? Did you ever see a gangster?"

And the Americans think, *This is quaint. There haven't been gangsters in Chicago since the 'twenties.*

There are gangsters in Chicago, and New York, Miami, all the American cities. Crime is rampant, and they're better armed than merely handguns. Their danger to the public stems more from their lawyers than their guns.

This climate of violence has caused not just an atmosphere in which blacks can be attacked, beaten, lynched, but one in which homosexuals can be singled out as a target group and be attacked, mugged, beaten, robbed, killed, with the apparent blessing of the President, the Secretary of State and the Moral Majority. The homosexuals have somehow been placed outside the law, by those Fundamentalists who feel the necessity to outlaw any phenomenon outside their experience.

The question of the homosexuals is not a sexual question; it is not a psychological question; it is a political question. No group of people may be singled out as a target group against whom violence may be employed with impunity. Otherwise, to that group will be added another group and another group and another group, until you have a fairly large segment of society on whom open season can be declared.

This country is too quick to forget; and the young are too badly educated to ever have known, or to be able to remember; but the Nazi regime began with the mercy killing of catatonic veterans from World War I, on the grounds that they had no life, they had no experience, they were "vegetables." Euthanasia was the first excuse for the Nazi killings. Then came the killing of the retarded, Mongoloid, crippled. Physical standards were set, and carried to such high extremes of perfection, that people could be killed for "badly modeled ears." Once the groundwork of social necessity for death had been laid, then came not just the Jews, but the gypsies and the homosexuals, the blacks, and any group the Nazis declared not to be a part of their plan for their new world.

I remember at the end of World War II, when we were the heroes of the world. Our soldiers went in, and released the people out of the concentration camps, and the people blessed them and threw flowers in their path. Our guys were the clean honest young heroes, helping to save the world. It was real beautiful when that was the one.

I have left this country. I left when Nixon was elected, and I left under Ronald Reagan's administration of California. But I came to the conclusion that I couldn't just leave this country. I had to stay here and inherit as much of it as was my lot to inherit, so that in the next generation my viewpoint would not go unsaid. I consider myself a patriot trying to bring a potentially great country into the cleanness and openness that I believed about it when I read about civics in the third grade, when I was in grammar school.

The conservatives don't want this country to become a cosmopolitan country. They resent the Cubans we have taken in; they resent the Vietnamese we have taken in; they resent the Cambodians we have taken in; they haven't finished resenting the Irish that we took in, or the blacks we took in, not to mention those we pressed in as slaves; they haven't finished resenting the Mexicans that come across the border. They resent all those folks.

I saw a change go down in New York City. Although the city had a tremendous number of blacks and Puerto Ricans in it, you never would see them on the news. If you looked at the television, you'd have to assume that everybody in that city was some kind of white guy with a short haircut. I watched the pressure become so great that New York City changed its character. When it changed its character is when Rockefeller and Lindsay bailed out: it was no longer the kind of place they could front for. It fell, some people think, into amateur hands. They think that the financial problems of New York City are because of the bumblings of the city government. But the financial problems of New York City are not necessarily merely the result of the bunglings of the city government; they are also that the heavy money folks won't invest money in New York City because New York

235

City is not run by the controlling establishment that they would like to have it run by. It is hard for New York City to have the same line of credit that any other city has, because it has become a Third World city-state. New York is no longer a White Anglo-Saxon Protestant city with just a few folks of other color to make it look liberal; it is now a true Third-World city state. It has newsmen, and women, of all colors and all languages, and hair, and naturals. You can look at the television in New York and tell that New York is a cosmopolitan city now.

The evolution that occurred in New York City is the natural result of the waves of immigrants that came to the United States. It used to be that boxers were Irish, and it was John L. Sullivan and Gentleman Jim Corbett. Then boxers became black. There was even a time when boxers were Jewish. Now boxers are Puerto Ricans. Boxers are now coming from smaller countries which are just now beginning to have immigration into the United States. As each of these waves of people stays in the United States longer, they climb up the only avenue of upward mobility available to them, which is the arts and the sports. Now the Polish people have been here long enough to come from Polish jokes to the fan at the playoff who held up a picture of the Polish Pope to bless Jaworski, the Polish quarterback.

In the same way that the Queen sends her message to England, the rulers of the United States send their messages to the people. President Roosevelt wanted us to feel that he cared about us, and that we could sit down and have a talk. He had his Fireside Chats, which were the standard for many years for close communication by a political figure in that rarefied sphere of the Presidency.

We were again having a message sent to us when President Nixon ordered the comic opera uniforms with the high shakos and the gold epaulets for the White House Guard. He was sending a message to the people that although *he* wore a "decent Quaker black suit", the position of the Presidency was to be considered as something like royalty, and that it would be surrounded with the perquisites and determiners of royalty, and the playing of "Hail to the Chief" in much the same way as "God Save the Queen."

President Carter sent us a message, especially in the early days, before he was told he was tacky, wearing Levi's, sweaters, Miz Roslyn photographed in a t-shirt advertising Jimmy Buffet and the Coral Reefers, trying to say that there really isn't any distance between the President and the people. But when times got rough for Jimmy Carter, he circled the wagons and hid behind his grey flannel crew like the rest of them.

Then, with the emergence of Ronald and Nancy Reagan as the First Couple, Mr. and Mrs. President, the specter of American royalty took flesh. Thorstein Veblen, in his explanations of human economics, spoke of the theory of conspicuous consumption: how, once a person's basic needs are met, the only way to show how rich they are and how much they have accomplished, is to *consume unnecessarily*. This was immediately the message sent from the White House.

"Well, it's okay; we're not going to use public money to redecorate everything (we'll just get our rich friends to kick in for us)." The message was close enough to arouse the late Publisher Loeb, of the Manchester *Union Leader* to intercept Mrs. Reagan's message, and question whether this was the message indeed intended for the country. It looked like, *If you got it, spend it.*

Publisher Loeb was acting more innocent than he really was. The message was deliberate and clear. It was to the rich middle class and upper class of the United States: *Continue to have fun. Do not be depressed by the Depression.* Don't allow the recession to keep you from being trendy, stylish.

The message to the United States is translated in a slightly different way to the rest of the world. The Third World hears it as, *Keep on fiddlin'. Rome is burning bright.*

Collectivity/Stewardship

We are the loyal opposition. We are loyal to most aspects of government in the U.S.

I reckon that the question of life and death and sovereignty of person is an innate personal matter, and cannot be bartered away for any more than the living generation at hand. I have not given that right to the government in my generation.

I am loyal to the Commonwealth. A system of distribution does not have to be state-owned or a state collective to be fair. A system of distribution such as we have could be fair as long as each person, at each stage in the transaction, didn't try to maximize the amount he could squeeze from his level. That's what, in the long run, contributes to high prices, short supply and shoddy goods.

UAW took a thirteen percent wage cut with Chrysler, the *de facto* behavior of a collective.

When the man sold the newspaper in Nashville and moved to Columbia and put his fifty-two million dollars in local banks, and went out and started building a bunch of stuff and employing a bunch of people, he was being collective. Columbia, as a whole, needed some money. For him to put his money in the Columbia banks loosened the credit so other people could borrow more money; the banks were more solid because they had more deposits. For him to employ more people added to the action; for him to buy up all that land and move all that business through the banks created more action, and hotted up the town. It was good for the county and the economy of Columbia. It was to his credit that he did that kind of thing with his money, rather than to centralize it by moving from Nashville to a bigger city and buying more expensive stuff. But he moved from Nashville to a *smaller* city, and actually performed the quasi-governmental function that the private sector is rumored to be able to perform.

He was a steward, and a bunch of money came through his hands and he made a decision about what he could benefit with it. He was making money on the deal, too, no sweat—not to mention getting to be the count of the county. But the county is quite grateful—otherwise they were going to be no 'count.

That's a place where the line between capitalism and communism is very fuzzy. It could have been expressed as *the local newspaper collective pledged itself to a larger national newspaper collective and transferred its assets to a local farming collective through the agency of Commissar What's-his-name, who moved to Columbia.* The same kind of transfer of funds could take place in pretty much the same way. You could call it communism or you could call it capitalism, but the same thing would have happened.

A Gratuitous Whack at Buckley

Maybe this isn't the proper place to do this, but I can't let this book go by without doing something that needs to be done. Since I have a little place to do it here, I might as well get on with it.

Has anybody noticed that Buckley has gone soft in the head? The way you can tell is that he crows so hard about the right wing finally taking over that he doesn't bother trying to prove anything, or be fair, or follow any of the rules of argument or philosophy. He uses his journal like a cheerleader, throwing to the wind whatever intellectual pretensions he may have had.

The low quality of argument that he allows in his magazine is noticeable in a pro-nuclear article in the June 12, 1981 issue. It says, "For nuclear power to be as dangerous as coal burning, we would have to have a meltdown every two weeks."

That's assuming they can contain a meltdown. But when they had only a partial meltdown at Three Mile Island, they had enough toxic emissions to cause the cows to be unable to birth their calves.

It says the containment would not be breached by a large quantity of TNT placed against its walls, or by an airplane flying into it, or by an aerial bomb. This is absolute nonsense. Other information is that a modern antitank shell could pierce the containment of a nuclear plant from two miles away. The government even publishes an unclassified handbook that tells how to get in with a screwdriver, bolt-cutter, and crowbar.

"To create enough steam to cause a steam explosion, the hundred tons of molten fuel would have to be effectively divided into pieces the size of small necklace beads, and all of it would have to strike the water within less than half a second."

It says that as if it were the most absolutely impossible condition that could conceivably occur. I submit that presently the Three Mile Island fuel is divided into pieces the size of small necklace beads immersed in water.

He argues that an increase from 17 to 17.5 per cent cancer rate would not be noticeable. What does that mean, would not be noticeable? Would not be noticeable to whom? To him, if he doesn't have cancer? Of course. But if he had one, it would be noticeable to him. It would be noticeable to anyone who had one.

The argument is that the only kind of radiation being added to the atmosphere is the design amount—the amount that would come out of a very well-run nuclear plant. He ignores the trucking aspect; there is one accident involving the transportation of radioactive materials every four days, on the average. One out of three accidents, releases radioactive materials to the environment somewhere in the United States.

He ignores the effects of the mining on the miners; these otherwise healthy men are dying at a very early age. In 1979, the U.S. Public Health Service found that 200 of 3,500 former miners surveyed over the past 30 years died from lung cancer. Under normal circumstances 40 such deaths could be expected in a group that size. In Australia, studies indicate that of 3,000 workers at the Radium Hill uranium mine from 1952-1962, 40.9% of the deaths of those working underground more than one year were from cancer, compared to 18.3% for those underground less than one year and 15% for above-ground uranium workers.

He ignores the effects of the tailings, which will continue to emit radioactivity for the next 3.5 billion years. He ignores the effects of waste disposal. He ignores the "swimming pools" full to overflowing with spent reactor fuel. There is all that potential for uncontained radiation, which he completely ignores in his article. He takes one, small, thin case of meltdown.

On the other hand, Dr. John W. Gofman, M.D., Ph.D., co-discoverer of Uranium-233 and of two processes for the isolation of plutonium, argues that:

"One must recognize that the low number of deaths listed for nukes is based on the industry's prediction that containment of radioactive poisons will be achieved with a miraculous 99.99 percent perfection. After presenting this prediction as if it were a fact, the industry compares it with coal, while conveniently assuming containment of coal poisons will be a flop. Thus, proof that nuclear power will be safe is manufactured out of thin air.

"The evidence shows that nuclear owner/operators do not believe their own safety claims. If they really did, they would not have insisted in 1957, 1967 and 1975 that either Congress pass a law (called the Price-Anderson Act) limiting the industry's liability for severe accidents, or else the industry would fold up, since it was not and is not willing to pay for the severe accident it claims will never happen. The Price-Anderson Act is a sign of severe insincerity behind the claims of nuclear power safety."

So it looks to me as if Buckley got himself a very sloppy nuke defender here. This is symptomatic of his whole magazine. Charlton Heston writes him about how you can't get peanut butter in hotels, and you can't get decent peanut butter overseas. "With brotherly affection, Chuck."

Then there is a whole page of a reader's response to Buckley's fudge recipe in which he mistakenly specified a tablespoon of salt. A fairly dumb move, but his rejoinder sizzles.

"Uh, er. Did I say a tablespoon of salt? I meant a couple of pinches of salt."

He has pages in which to give and get ego strokes. On substantive matters, he simply lies. Buckley's comment on the I.R.A. hunger strikers is,

"There are no political prisoners in the United Kingdom, or for that matter in the U.S., France, or the rest of our democracies, unsatisfactory though they may be in other respects."

Now there is a blanket statement of nonsense. There are political prisoners. I was a political prisoner. There are black, Indian, and many other political prisoners in the United States itself.

Perhaps it is naive of me to look at so frankly partisan a journal as *National Review* and expect any form of fairness. Buckley should just admit that he is a house organ for the wealthy, and go on ahead and get about the business of propaganda. He should give up the pretense that he is smart and that he somehow gets to publish this journal because of his outstanding intelligence, rather than because it pleases the kind of people who have money to support their viewpoint.

Here's a perfect example of the kind of thing he does to distort events and link people together.

"Before his election, Francois Mitterand said the rupture of diplomatic relations with Pinochet's Chile is for us a symbolic act which underlines the closeness that France has for democracy and justice.

"Mitterand, a member of the Socialist International who supports the El Salvador rebels, got especially warm greetings on his election from Fidel Castro and the Sandinista junta in Nicaragua."

I'm sure there were formal greetings from the whole spectrum of government. Because Mitterrand was down on Chile for where Chile is at, they immediately have to hook him up to Castro and the Sandinista junta.

These clips are examples of the kind of fawning that Buckley does to pay his dues:

"Former national Democratic chairman Robert Strauss knows a pro when he sees one, even in the other camp. 'This fellow Reagan,' he says, 'is a one man band, and his White House staff is simply spectacular. Reagan has done what he said he would do, and has done it far better than I conceived he would do it.' "

"Califano, Carter's secretary of Health, Education and Welfare, concurs:

" 'In political acumen and leadership, Reagan is far more effective than any other President since LBJ.' "

Their humor is incredible. They have a cartoon of a woman being stabbed to death upon a sacrificial altar, with the caption, "Serves her right. She was always whining about women not being allowed to participate in the services."

What they are really good at, however, is misdirection. I don't want to argue any more how much radioactivity is going to escape from the containment of a nuclear power plant and what the likelihood is for that. Those odds, while high enough to be worried about, are not really the shockingly high odds that we all have to be afraid of.

The real nuclear danger that we have to fear is the fact that we have twenty thousand hydrogen bombs scattered around in various submarines and missile silos all around the United States, and the Russians have almost an equal amount. We have enough radioactive stuff being handled by half-trained soldiers all over the world that there is a real possibility of an air burst of H-bomb level anywhere in the world at any time. They have already dropped several H-bombs out of airplanes by accident, and only flukes prevented them from going off and actually exploding fission/fusion.

Howard Moreland disclosed that the "H-bomb secret" was not a secret (and not even mysterious) in *The Progressive*, for which he was censored by the Federal government and threatened with life imprisonment. As he points out, it's not even the question of all those missiles and all those silos. But an H-bomb need only be as big as a small garbage can. The real missile of delivery which we have to fear is not the MX missile or the Trident sub or the Strategic Air Command bomber, but the rent-a-car. Any car or truck coming across any border from anywhere could drive into any city in the United States and take an H-bomb into the center of the city that would be powerful enough to blow a crater the size of

Yankee Stadium, and we wouldn't even know who did it.

I understand that there have been tactical reasons for separating the anti-nuclear power movement from the anti-nuclear weapons movement because it is thought that the anti-nuclear power movement could go farther without being stopped, because it wouldn't alarm the war machine as fast. But I think we should just stand up and say the truth: the leak out of an old melted down nuke is one thing, but the possibility of proliferation and the obvious dangers of atomics floating into the hands of terrorists and small third-world dictator countries has been caused by the United States' and Germany's and England's and Canada's and Russia's attitude about nuclear power and nuclear war, and they have put the world in hostage, in a much more serious way than *National Review* would ever dare to hint at. He already has the argument in his own court, because he gets to just talk about some old leaky nuke.

This is the sort of absolutely missing the point of the real issue that is Buckley's real skill. That's what *National Review* does, is very skillfully miss all of the points in such a way as to seem almost plausible.

That is the difference between *National Review* and a journal like *Akwesasne Notes*, which makes the points again and again. In *Akwesasne Notes*, what you can find is good research that has been carefully done in depth on serious subjects that affect the real health, life and welfare of living people. There are reports on Native People from first hand sources. They have their axe (or tomahawk: forgive me Katsi) to grind too but they let their subject matter carry the weight and do not try to fool their readers or mold their minds.

The difference between *National Review* and *Akwesasne Notes* is a result of the way they live. The publishers of *Akwesasne Notes* have been publishing a high-quality journal for a year and a half, surrounded by various armed vigilantes and state troopers. This has sharpened their wits. They put out a truly intellectual journal. The American Indians have an intellectual tradition. *Akwesasne Notes* shows that there are other people who are intelligent and who have great philosophies, who are not necessarily Christian or Greco-Roman. The American Indians are some of these.

This journal is so much better than *National Review* that it would be worth anyone's while who wanted to make a serious and honest literary comparison of them to get a copy of *National Review* at your local newsstand and send a couple of dollars to *Akwesasne Notes*, Mohawk Nation, via Rooseveltown, NY 13683, and ask for a copy of *Akwesasne Notes*, and compare them for yourself. You will be able to see the difference between a house organ that is paid for with multinational money to propagandize their issues, which in the final analysis is not any different than a soap commercial, and *Akwesasne Notes*, which is one of the few papers in the United States that is in any way related to the tradition of freedom of the press that is symbolized by Peter Zenger and the First Amendment to the Constitution.

The New Protestants

A friend of mine who is an American Indian who has been holding the FBI and the state police at bay for a year and a half, told me to stay out of politics. And I hear him, too. There was a time when we first came to Lewis County in Tennessee and decided we wouldn't vote so we wouldn't disturb the balance of power. But when we heard word that they were going to legislate us into being a trailer park and say we didn't have a license, we went down and registered to vote. We are now sixteen-some per cent of the vote in our county.

Reagan only carried Tennessee by two thousand votes. The American electoral college system is terrible. If a state goes one way by fifty votes out of several million, all that state's electoral votes go to one candidate. In Tennessee, it was two thousand. We have six hundred votes. If seven hundred votes had been different, our vote would have been pivotal.

I know the difference between Democrats and Republicans is pretty slim. But in Latin America, when they knew the Republicans were going to win, they started shooting Indians faster. That's enough of a difference for me, for a start.

Then, we need to reform the party so it more fully represents its constituents. The basis for the party is going to have to be ecological and human, rather than based on personalities.

I would rather not be involved in politics. But I don't see how we can turn our backs on it at this point.

I remember when the United States were the good guys. I don't like it that we aren't the good guys right now. That's my country. I don't have any other citizenship. No other country will let me stay; they keep sending me back to this one. This is the one where I speak the language.

I do not feel like letting my country be taken over by a minority of people who are so ignorant as to mess over the rest of the world in our name. I resent that being done in my name as an American. I have to become involved because that is the only way I can stop it from happening.

The Constitution is a liberating document against an Establishment. People act like the Constitution describes the United States as it is now. Actually, the U.S. of today is but one of many possible United States, all well within the ground rules of the same Constitution. The United States could be full of small collective bubbles until it was mostly collective, without changing a word in the Constitution.

The Constitution is not a static document. It has no allegiance to the status quo. It refers to principles of right and justice, and urges that the public apply those principles in their own defense.

The coalition that fell apart when the Republicans won, the coalition put together by Roosevelt that lasted all these years must be replaced with something. The people who understand that must get out in the precincts and the small districts and the counties and get into politics, and start building a ground movement. Start building a party. Don't wait for a candidate to come along. No matter who comes along, King Arthur couldn't get it if he didn't have a party.

Dig Teddy Kennedy's speech at the convention. He pointed out that it is the Democratic Party's ideal to help those who are not in power. It's the reason the Republicans have, as a party ritual, to not call the Democrats the Democratic Party. No "in" Republican ever says "The Democratic Party." He always says "The Democrat Party." But it is the Democratic Party's own statement about itself that it *is* the Democratic Party.

Coalition politics has to be idealistic. The thing about

coalition politics that makes one sick is *expedient* coalition politics: How are we gonna get the Jewish vote? How are we gonna get the Italian vote? But the fact remains that if the small groups do not have some kind of a coalition that is based around their very smallness and vulnerability, they will remain small and vulnerable—or squished.

There are not enough black people in this country to move it. There are not enough intellectual idealistic college kids to move it. There are not enough hippies to move it. There are not enough homosexuals to move it. There are not enough feminists to move it. But it must be moved.

You have to coalesce around the highest ideal, rather than the lowest. The highest ideal is that in a country like this, the machinery for the protection of the small must be kept in use at all times, or the small will not be protected. It is the assumption that people can come together, demonstrate, petition, assemble, etc., in this country. When the assemblies are confined so that nothing ensues from them, and when it is foreknown that the petitions are not going to be listened to, then no redress of grievances exists.

If a party in power does not have to listen to demonstrations, press, etc., and can just plow along doing its thing because the critics do not have the power to do anything, one is faced with two evils. The greater of those evils is revolution. The lesser is coalition.

We have to rebuild the Democratic party to the ideals which it was supposed to embody: it was the party of the small groups who couldn't face the large interest groups by themselves. It was supposed to be the hippies and the black people. All those people who had a hard time defending themselves, were supposed to get together. It worked. We have to get that back. We need it, and the world needs it desperately.

I don't think this is even political. I think this is the hard kind of thinking you have to do that is harder than thinking about Armageddon.

The last election was won with about twenty-six per cent of the electorate: fifty-one per cent voted, so twenty-six per cent was all it took for a majority. We have been content to let our people go into office with smaller and smaller actual real mandates, just so they won the election, until now we are in a position where half the people don't vote. The reason half the people don't vote is because they feel powerless. They feel powerless in the face of the world they are living in right now.

They have to jump right in, start participating, vote, meet other people, talk over issues, try to meet information sources that have good stuff, try to educate themselves about what newspapers or magazines or news shows carry truthful information and viewpoints.

The exhortation to register to vote and all of that may seem to some people to be a not-very-revolutionary sounding remedy for such horrendous and dangerous-sounding ills; but as loaded as the deck is in the United States, it is one of the few countries where they let you in the game.

We can't waste our revolutionary energy in squawking about the loaded dice; we have to just come on so strong as to overcome that—which is not as impossible as it seems at first glance, because we have a tremendous amount of justice in our viewpoint. The true religious viewpoint is to understand that money does not buy everything, no matter what it may look like. In the long run, money doesn't make it. If you believe that, then you can't just quit and roll over because you're out-moneyed. That's not the significant factor.

The right-wing presence has won the right, by the elective process, to try its experiment. Although the experiment is not only doomed, but ruinously costly, the best thing to do is let it do its thing while you organize. The mistakes it makes are so apparent that it loses support daily. Its greatest number of constituents was on the day of the inauguration, and it has lost steadily and constantly since then, as a result of its own actions. We need to point this out, comment on this and show that it was foretold.

At the same time, we need to organize grassroots so we can make changes in the long run. We need to realize that being moderate is not being chicken; being moderate is recognizing that nobody likes being oppressed, and a reasonable desire for justice will dictate that the things we do are not so extreme as to cause it to be overturned the next time the pendulum swings.

We need to use our influence not only to regain constituency in the actual government, but to stabilize the situation for the sake of everyone, not just parties. We have to resist the tendency to set our phrases into more extreme shades of our values than we really feel. I have seen young college civil rights-ers who were motivated by social justice rather than politics, say and speak jargon far to the left of their actual stance, satirically, as a conversational way of expressing a strongly held view. They just talked bad because they knew it annoyed the Administration.

I see the right wing doing the same thing. The right wingers espouse causes farther to the right than where they really live, for the sake of amplifying or expressing how strongly they hold their views. To a casual observer, the passionate rhetoric of Democrats and Republicans can scan like communists and fascists. But this country isn't really made out of communists and fascists, and it really is one of the more economically democratic countries in the world, if only by the accident of our awesome natural resources. This political system and this media system in interaction create a climate of tolerance such that even in 1981, we are one of the sanctuaries of the world. Refugees even fleeing the United States' wrath flee *to* the United States. That is to say, this country, this system is workable enough to be worth saving.

I don't want my American Indian friends to think that I endorse the sovereignty of the United States over the American Indian nations because of this, because I don't. I don't think it would diminish the sovereignty of the United States if it granted sovereignty to the native tribes within its borders on some kind of an equal constitutional basis to both parties, as was specified in the Great Two Row Wampum, which sealed a treaty of equality. This wampum showed the Indians' canoe and the white men's ship as two equal rows of beads of the same size and length.

Gandhi remains as relevant as he was when he was alive, because the force of Truth is the only force that we are allowed. You can know the truth, but then you have to build a microphone, like one's own golden horn.

The old Protestants were people of conscience in Europe—the Lutherans, Quakers and all those who came from Europe to this country for sanctuary. They were protesting that they didn't have control over their worship, or the freedom of their life. Those Protestants were coming out of the Church of England or various European authoritarian church structures. The New Protestants are living under the Constitution, which is supposed to guarantee them the right to certain human freedoms, those that were fought for, for which people left everything in Europe and came to this country. These Protestants, for the most part, are similar to the old Protestants in that the old Protestants didn't want to quit being religious, but they wanted more self-determination. We don't want to quit living under the Constitution; but we want the Constitution to mean the thing it was intended to mean, whether it practically ever meant that or not.

We assume a Constitution that is a protective document. We assume that if we find out that it's not a protective document, that that was obviously a mistake, and it should be amended so as to be a protective document.

Our protest is not to pervert the system or divert the system, but to make the system fulfill itself.

That is why we protest: not to break the law, but to fulfill it. We assume that the law represents the people; and if the law doesn't represent the people, it should be amended. If this is not the assumption under which we are all doing this, then no one owes any allegiance to this government or to any other.

Index